COMPOUND CAPITALISM

SLAYING THE DRAGON OF DEBT

Walton Cook

Compound Capitalism: Slaying the Dragon of Debt

Copyright © 2018 by Walton Cook

Second Edition 2018

Design by Rick Brandt

Manufactured in the United States of America

ISBN 978-0-9709832-1-3

To Barbara, my wife

Contents

Compound Capitalism: Raising the Curtain

Preface

The focus of this modern performance is on revitalizing capitalism by acts providing secure funding for **Retirement Income Security (RIS), Retirement Healthcare Security (RHS) and Lifetime Educational Support (LES).** The difference in staging this capitalist revival is the better uses of compound interest and younger and better educated talent in key roles. Look for your name in the program. *Compound Capitalism* as a performance will return almost $1 million to every new U.S. citizen born or naturalized after its opening day legislative implementation. Each new citizen will receive direct benefits, two-thirds of that million dollars inheritable by the account owner's selected beneficiaries. The performance will remove the accurate description of ***"Unsustainable!"*** from present Social Security and Retirement Medicare futures.

You will receive a ticket and your role in *Compound Capitalism* in advance so you can better participate in and also enjoy the show, perhaps even earn a leading role, or otherwise lend a hand to new and fellow citizens in the actor audience. No more *"waiting in the wings."* It is a record setting production in which the best abilities of all its performers must be better utilized. You will finally see your name in the credits—if not in lights.

In crucial ways, this performance is more personal, psychological and philosophic than economic, as the primary importance of human capital surpasses other considerations.

Compound Capitalism asks what kind of a government would think enough of the potential performances of its newest citizens to invest in tickets for their individual lifetime accomplishment, productivity and security, and in advance—not yet knowing who among us are to become the more talented? Such governing leaders would also have recognized that no ticket holders are identical in their genetic, financial, environmental, emotional and cultural heritages.

Almost certainly, it would take the kind of leadership who knew instinctively that opportunity and incentive are the keys to innovation and for the long run stability and well being of what we see as a special form of democratic capitalistic government—America. They would also feel it in their bones that shareholders with skin-in-the-game always perform in more positive ways.

What kind of artistic director is so confident of the end result of his motivational and teaching skills that he will give important roles in his production to actors whose skills he has not yet seen in dress rehearsal? Perhaps the only kind of director that would do this knows the script by heart, backward and forward, tests it regularly, knows it is rock solid and that many players with the right encouragement can easily become a choice for star billing. Stars are born regularly.

That is the case, too, with a government that has started off with a director's marked-up script that says that it is "... *of the people, by the people and for the people.*"

That kind of government is willing to give new citizens important roles to play, because it knows in advance that new citizens have already paid for their tickets, either by having earned the right of performance through past practice and rehearsal, or have inherited the cultural right from the sweat and tears of present and former citizens with performance equity history, although too often without appropriate past billing in the list of credits.

We are talking about former or present taxpayers, of course, those who pass their mantle of shareholding on the basis of membership in a particular and unique company and belief system, their evolving culture of democratic free market capitalism. So that the show will go on, better than ever, continuing its world record run; future actors are best given parts suited to their talents, choice and opportunity, and sufficient front-row seats are to be held in reserve at the box office. Emphasis will be on learning new dialog— new words for the times.

Compound Capitalism also gains applause from attention to where steady new box office revenues can be found. We call this supporting music *Big Bills Left on the Sidewalk.* **It's played from the pit by the symphony orchestra backing the performance.**

Most of all, *Compound Capitalism* creates dynamic and exciting new dialog regarding responsible government and citizenship; ideas in words that highly regarded economist Dr. Paul Romer interchangeably calls both recipes and *'non-rival'* goods. According to Dr. Romer, *'non-rival goods'* are ideas that can be used at the same time (or at any time), like a recipe, and by as many people as wish to use it; and in any number of places, while neither reducing its supply nor diminishing the utility or value of the idea to any person.

This is contrasted against *'rival goods,'* ideas or recipes whose utility is diminished by the scarcity caused by their use or restricted, (even though temporarily), by the existence of monopoly powers granted by patents and/or intellectual property rights that limit the rights of others.

Every generation has perceived the limits to growth that finite resources and undesirable side effects would pose if no new recipes or ideas were discovered. And every generation has historically underestimated the potential for finding new recipes and ideas. We consistently fail to grasp how many ideas remain to be discovered. Possibilities do not add up. They multiply.

—Dr. Paul Romer from The Concise Encyclopedia of Economics

And recipes, knowledge and opportunities compound, one thought leading to others—and more, meshing; then separating and reintegrating anew—and anew again. Even words and language take on new meanings.

And so, the multiplication of ideas and compounding of their values, as well as wealth created by compounding financial interest, are the recurring plot-lines of *Compound Capitalism*. The subtitle, *Slaying the Dragon of Debt*, is a sub-plot gaining constant excitement and applause. (You will look good dressed as a brave dragon-slaying knight.)

Remember that it's not only the multiplication of ideas, but also the compounding of information, of new interests, and even multiplying the meaning of old words, words that we now use in newer ways and in newer interlocking relationships. Just a few years ago, who ever heard of the *Internet*, or *Google* or soon, inexpensively and easily getting your DNA genome sequenced?

Our audiences will look at some of the latest thinking in economics, science, technology, taxation, psychology, history, political science, diplomacy and governance.

We will explore the necessity to vastly expand the evolving basis of democratic capitalism, the concept of entrepreneurial, innovative and citizen participation and ownership of a fully widespread shareholding society. It is needed. FDIC reports that 17 million Americans do not have a bank account and 62% have less than $1000 in a savings account. We contend throughout *Compound Capitalism* that America's current 42% shareholder equity ownership falls shamefully short of the 100% participation goal of a great democratic and market capitalist society—and of a self-renewing American Dream. It is a dream yet unfulfilled.

"… that government of the people, by the people and for the people, shall not perish from the earth." —Abraham Lincoln: Gettysburg, PA—November 19, 1863

One wonders why leadership often fails to use alternate and renewable energy sources that are already easily available? Largely, it's the failure to think of more meanings of the same words. *Compound Capitalism* will not fail to recognize that fresh money can be a renewable energy source—a fresh definition of energy. We all feel the daily need for alternate sources of energy, and even more critical is the 'renewable' part.

To find renewable financial energy, we will explore other political implications of *Big Bills Left on the Sidewalk,* the famous paper by the late economist, Mancur Olson, Jr.

Olson's paper describes two economics professors walking down the street (one a full professor and the other an assistant professor) and coming upon a $100 bill lying on the sidewalk. As the junior professor bends to pick up the money, the full professor haughtily remarks:

"If that were real, someone else would have already picked it up."

We will walk together down America's Main Streets, Wall Street and other streets of the world, which will lead us to the discovery of many more *Big Bills Left on the Sidewalk*— very real bills indeed, but much bigger bills!

We will suggest ways to utilize an unrecognized debt reduction opportunity as the ongoing incentive to drive a innovative spirit of excitement into the present and hope and cooperation into the future—far into the future.

Among the topics covered will be questions like: How to find new sources of long-term capital investment and savings? Where to look for it and to know how and when we are looking at substantial societal gain? How much gain might there be? Will we know it when we see it? Who says it is really there? When might we expect to get it? What do we need to do next?

Compound Capitalism will suggest formulas to prevent large increases in personal and national savings from becoming new and unregulated political bonanzas for reckless government spending. We will recommend precautions to ensure reducing debt as a legislative priority, so as to prevent corruption, crony capitalism, regional powers and entrenched interest groups from defeating the goals of responsible national savings and steady economic growth.

Opportunities covered will be the growing debt crisis, reducing and then eliminating that debt, Social Security, Medicare, Medicaid, K-12, vocational and university education, national security, international aid, tax reform, immigration reform, agriculture, technology, biology and biotechnology, responsive and responsible political leadership, citizen responsibility, and redirection of influence from special interest groups.

How will that change the way we think? We will try to incorporate our genetic, psychological and cultural heritages, what cognitive psychologist Dr. Steven Pinker says about what we were born with in his thoughtful book, *The Blank Slate*, along with other insights from another path breaking Pinker book, *The Stuff of Thought*—and then, as explained by Judith Rich Harris, how *"by choice or by luck"* peer group memberships influence our socialization in *The Nurture Assumption: Why Children Turn Out the Way They Do.*

Why these psychological and genetic insights are now so important is that *Compound Capitalism* attempts to add to the heritable legacy we started life with—adding new *'memes'* and valuable cultural inheritances, so that both our children and ourselves turn out, in very key ways, much better than we might have previously imagined—perhaps even hoped for, including improving our powers to cooperate with, reciprocate and reward each other.

Included are lines and exchanges from prominent leaders in media, academia, political science, scientific research, history, and national security. You will recognize leaders who have been supportive of finding *Big Bills Left on the Sidewalk.*

But most of all, we will learn a new master performance recipe, how increasing the number of shareholders in The American Dream to 100% of American citizens will finally and fully compliment both citizen and leadership visions of a truly participating and cooperating democratic society, a social network connecting every American, fully using the productivity of all our human resources. The chapter recipes contain the critical ingredients—most of which are available to all. This is *Compound Capitalism*.

It's curtain time!

Chapter 1. Compound Capitalism: Compound Interest and Compound Interests

"The most powerful force in the universe is compound interest."—Albert Einstein, Nobel Prize, 1921

The *American Heritage Dictionary* defines compound interest as: Interest computed over time on the accumulated interest as well as upon the original invested principal.

Compound Interest Tables
at 6.3 %, 6.5%, 6.8% and 7.3%

Account Holder's Invested Value				
Effects of Compounding Interest on Initial Investment of $8,000				
		Interest Rate		
Year	6.30%	6.50%	6.80%	7.30%
10	$15,885	$16,234	$16,771	$17,707
20	29,777	31,043	33,041	36,662
30	55,818	59,359	65,094	75,908
40	104,632	113,506	128,242	157,167
50	196,134	217,043	252,648	325,413
60	367,657	415,027	497,740	673,767
67	538,830	615,657	751,884	1,049,034

In other words, if you had an account with money or invested capital in it, so long as it was left untouched in the account, the interest earned on the principal savings would be regularly added to the original investment and the original investment would continue to grow by adding that earned interest and growth to your account, over and over. **And since this adding happens automatically, most people are surprised to learn that even modest sums like $8,000 for an extended period of time, shown in the chart above, can become amazingly large, even at conservative average rates of growth over long periods of time, like 6.5%. The return at age 67 is $615,657. That's $77 for every $1 invested.**

A financial account can consist of assets that are representations of money as well as actual money. Good examples are stocks and bonds. The essence is that institutions; a government, a city, a hospital—as well as financial institutions and corporations, also have regular needs for invested capital. For use of this capital, they sometimes pay fixed interest rates, others may pay dividends, which are their investment's equivalent of interest. In addition, in the case of corporate stock they, too, can also increase in value and continuously roll earnings back into the shareholder original account. In the case of a pension type investment, it can also accumulate tax free, being taxed only when received as income by the account owner.

Where discussions of compound interest can easily fall short is by limiting one's mental vision to only the financial definition. Although most people don't realize how fast assets grow when subjected to compound interest, they probably don't give much thought at all to the compounding of other interests that are much closer to our daily lives. What other kinds of interests compound rapidly?

Almost everyone has heard of Moore's law. Intel co-founder Gordon Moore is a legend, a visionary. His now famous prediction states that the number of transistors on a chip will double about every two years. So far, he is right. Intel has kept that pace for over forty years, also providing more functions at significantly lower cost per function. That's compound interest, the computer's capacity to multiply its powers!

Now consider the incredible growth of knowledge, not just that we know more, write more and more of us do it, but that there has also been a data and knowledge compounding so incredible a rate that we double the world's recorded data every three years. That's compounding many areas of interest—and all at 1/33,000th of our species time on earth.

Then there's the daily compounding of general information, whether or not we call it the news cycle or new knowledge. When was it possible, up till now, to see and hear history in the making, whether war, disaster, discovery or diplomacy? We learn more about others and the world in a day than was previously possible in months or years.

Opinion vs. fact is also compounded. We learn very quickly about what works and what doesn't, because new ideas and results are studied by more people, people knowledgeable about making rational evaluations and then sharing their conclusions.

Compound Capitalism will also suggest that states of mind, how people feel about themselves and others also spread rapidly. We see enough of this in fads, fashion, and foods to conclude that more lasting human preferences also spread quickly and widely. That leads to the question of what human emotions would one choose to share most widely, if the opportunity to do so were provided? What if the best human interests were compounded?

Chapter 2. The American Dream

Historian James Truslow Adams popularized the thought *"American Dream"* in his 1931 book *Epic of America.*

The American Dream is that dream of a land in which life should be better and richer and fuller for every man, with opportunity for each according to ability or achievement. It is a difficult dream for the European upper classes to interpret adequately, also too many of us ourselves have grown weary and mistrustful of it. It is not a dream of motor cars and high wages merely, but a dream of social order in which each man and each woman shall be able to attain to the fullest stature of which they are innately capable, and be recognized by others for what they are, regardless of the fortuitous circumstances of birth or position.

But there are other versions, all similar.

"We hold these truths to be self-evident, that all men are created equal, that they are endowed by their Creator with certain unalienable Rights, that among these are Life, Liberty and the pursuit of Happiness." Thomas Jefferson, The Declaration of Independence,1776

"I rejoice in a belief that intellectual light will spring up in the dark corners of the earth; that freedom of enquiry will produce liberality of conduct; that mankind will reverse the absurd position that the many were, made for the few; and that they will not continue slaves in one part of the globe, when they can become freemen in another." George Washington, draft of First Inaugural Address, 1789

"... that we here highly resolve that these dead shall not have died in vain; that this nation, under God, shall have a new birth of freedom; and that this government of the people, by the people,

for the people, shall not perish from the earth." Abraham Lincoln, November 19, 1863.

"I have a dream that one day this nation will rise up and live out the true meaning of its creed: We hold these truths to be self-evident: that all men are created equal." I have a dream that one day on the red hills of Georgia the sons of former slaves and the sons of former slave owners will be able to sit down together at a table of brotherhood." Martin Luther King, August 28, 1963

Chapter 3. Capitalism as You Know It & Other So-Called Capitalisms

The condition of possessing capital; the position of a capitalist; a system which favors the existence of capitalists. *Capitalism, n: Oxford English Dictionary*

In the historic drama of homo sapiens, in which we all now play our part on stage, the curtain of democratic free-market capitalism has not been opened for very long.

Assuming a human species starting point of 130,000 years ago, our ancestors used most of the first 120,000 years as hunter-gatherers.

Then, somewhere close to 12,000—15,000 years ago, we started to become farmers. The first signs of commerce may have appeared shortly after, in forms of the simple trading of skills, concepts or artifacts. Approximately 8,000 years ago our spoken language was first expressed through writing.

Although trading and writing increased rapidly, it was not until writing had given us capitalism's founding document, Adam Smith's *Wealth of Nations* in 1776 and with it the founding of the United States in the same year, that the ascent toward the democratic free-market capitalism of the present began.

So we have had a short go of it with selling goods and services, and the rules keep changing; from the exploitive models set by the Dutch and British East India Companies, then to the more contemporary U.S. monopoly capitalists of the 19th and early 20th Centuries, and now to the present global integration of markets.

Although we have much to learn from study, this is not a history book, even of economic history. For that, we recommend Niall Ferguson's *Colossus* and *Ascent of Money*.

In the first chapters of their excellent book, *Good Capitalism, Bad Capitalism*, economist William Baumol and his co-authors outline four major types of capitalism. They are:

State Guided Capitalism, in which government tries to guide the market, most often by supporting particular industries that it expects to become "winners."

Oligarchic Capitalism, in which the bulk of the power and wealth is held by a small group of individuals and families.

Big-firm Capitalism, in which the most significant economic activities are carried out by giant established enterprises.

Entrepreneurial Capitalism, in which a significant role is played by small, innovative firms.

Dr. Baumol and his co-authors outline some of the major benefits and disadvantages of the first three and conclude that it takes a combination of the last two forms, **Big Firm Capitalism** and **Entrepreneurial Capitalism** to succeed in a world of compounding ideas, knowledge, science and technology.

A central theme throughout their book discusses ideas and innovation expressed in action through opportunity, innovation, education, and (R&D) research and development, also later themes of *Compound Capitalism*.

So what may they not have considered? Could some other capitalism be overlooked, or a word defined differently? The answer in advance is yes!

Perhaps they are the same kinds of words, but still in need of more nuanced interpretations?

What many overlook is that America has not had as long a democratic free-market capitalist history as is believed. What the state can do is to determine just what kind of institution it is—and it did. In fact, during the pre-Civil War era and afterward, until after WWI, the United States was a high protective tariff nation, with little claim in reality to being *'free-market.'* Therefore, neither the words many today too easily call *'democratic free-market,'* has been long so described. The newer word *'globalized,'* is not an accurate term for describing either the prior or the present world economies.

Since, *'globalized'* has now been mentioned, our view of that word is that it is not descriptive of what is taking place anywhere in the world today. What is global in our view is the merging of markets and cultures. Better to use the term global market integration to describe the economic aspects of change, as the facts also reflect that most every nation is free-market and capitalist only in terminology, rather than in reality. For example, protectionism abounds, in the EU for mostly agricultural products and in China and India for a large number of goods manufactured by industries their nations protect in the interest of gaining market shares over time on the basis of price. The respect for rule-of-law and protection of intellectual property rights is also widely divergent.

Truth be told, there are few aspects of either service or industrial industries that are close to being a 'level playing field' throughout the world; wages, working conditions, safety standards, environmental controls, employee benefits or freedom of movement come nowhere close to standards observed in the United States.

For all these reasons, nations are more likely to adopt policies that emphasize domestic needs and domestic politics much more than considerations related to free-markets. And they do. Markets are more and more integrated, to be sure, but the world is not flat, as suggested, but is fully one of hill and dale, mountain and valley.

'Integration' is a more accurate word barometer, and we advocate that the better course of political valor is to adjust policy and adopt policy most likely to meet the needs of a nation's own citizenry—interests first domestic—then global.

Another shared misgiving is that our definition of capitalism has close competitors. One could agree that *'global economic integration'* exists, but only in the sense that the trade of goods and services is worldwide. That is much different than 'democratic free-market capitalism.'

We have serious competition over actions, but not over words. Nations like Russia, China, India, Brazil and others are competitors, but both our cultural heritage and our style of capitalism is far different. Global trading does not define capitalism, only marketing. Other nations employ more authoritarian management styles than does the U.S. model. In other clearly structural ways they also differ, and are often dictatorships, oligarchies, monarchies; all authoritarian—doing what they do to first benefit ruling elites before their own people. Nations manipulate their currencies for their own benefit, steal the intellectual properties of others, violate international rule-of-law—the list goes on. Even in the West, some in outward capitalist dress remain intellectually and politically state dominated, some others socialist states, both in orientation and in fact.

Additionally, some market competitors mix and match several of the preceding elements. Despite the differences, however, almost all are in agreement on selling worldwide.

The hope is that differences in separate systems must not be allowed to alienate any of us from prosperity. The best we can do is to make our model one in which we can take pride and that also sets a moral tone worth noticing and repeating. As the leading Western economy, our model must set a new standard of rules-of-the-game excellence that we hope others will copy.

We must encourage American leadership to simultaneously engage both large and interconnected worldwide market competition, but with recognition and favor toward domestic needs, both without tacitly embracing undemocratic globalization, and at the same time, making it prosperous to focus on mutual cooperation with others and for them to work more easily with us. *Compound Capitalism* favors rational integration, not globalization.

Different nations have vastly different domestic needs. We are too large a nation to ignore such facts. We cannot outsource everything. First, it is more important that we achieve the highest standards of which we are domestically capable, lest premature concern with conformity to lesser values waste our energies.

As mentioned in the preface of this book, what stands out as a critical missing element in almost every recent book, (no matter how astute otherwise) is a failure to discuss capitalism as we have known it to date as incomplete, a still evolving model—a work-in-progress open to a more inclusive form of revitalized capitalism. We need skin-in-the-game shareholders. The capacity for capitalism to evolve as other ideas evolve has been ignored in such books as French author Thomas Piketty's *Capital in the 21st Century*. That is more than a small oversight.

We have talked about the meanings of words and taking advantage of differences in similar words, when the same words very often describe different or rapidly changing circumstances. Capitalism=Evolution. The two very different words can compliment each other.

Chapter 4. Compound Capitalism Evolution: The New American Dream

"Every new citizen will have a new inherited birthright. Every citizen will be recognized as a common shareholder in the enterprise of the world's greatest democratic capitalist republic, and new shareholding will be represented by heritable financial assets—actual shares in trust fund investments made through both citizen tax dollars and through capitalizing other untapped savings opportunities. Each citizen will also have significant increases in both health and educational assets. This dream is a grateful nation's gift to citizens, an inherent belief that the citizen's future productivity contributions and freedom, including freedom of imagination, diligence and cooperation with fellow citizen shareholders will increase the life, liberty and pursuit of happiness for all."—Walton Cook, August 1, 2016

A New American Dream

Every American schoolchild has heard stories of the courage and struggles to conquer our frontier, the courage of battles lost and won, even recorded events of many less noble outcomes, which in honestly looking back, little or no pride can or should be taken.

Nonetheless, in the balanced cumulative historical view, we still like to think of ourselves as the founders did, as a *'City on a Hill.'* Perhaps what historian Steven Ambrose called *Undaunted Courage* must now come to realistic grips with a need for a new kind of grit, a kind needed to meet not only the challenges of competitors, but also those of a growing current National Debt and a future of unfunded liability called *'unsustainable.'* We must replace that offensive word, *'unsustainable,'* once again, with *"Undaunted."*

Compound Capitalism presents a means to change the inheritance of every new citizen, engineering a "shareholder gene" into every new American. It is through this anticipated non-random memetic mutation, horizontal intellectual transfer, although a cultural one, that we hope to make permanent substantial heritable assets. In so doing, *Slaying the Dragon of Debt* is an essential element of our *'hope for the future process.'*

Compound Capitalism is the New American Dream. In order to make it a waking reality, we must begin with a multiplication of citizen capitalists within a very short time frame. We can realize this virtually overnight. Given the fact that less than half of all U.S. citizens presently own shareholder ownership interests as personal assets, a strong move toward correcting that missing element seems in order.

We need 100% capitalists, all with skin-in-the-game!

Compound Capitalism **will first capitalize the existing human assets by utilizing long term compound interest to maximize both individual and collective growth potential with two invested sums, one of $8,000 into each citizen's Retirement Income Security (RIS) trust, and one of $4,000, into a Retirement Healthcare Security (RHS) trust, invested at the birth of each legal citizen or at the naturalization of legal immigrants. (A further cumulative $12 billion annually will be provided to (LES) Lifetime Educational Security benefiting all living Americans.**

The sum in the first trust (RIS)is fully heritable, and at a 6.5% interest rate, represents a $615,000 shareholder asset at age 67, the present retirement age for those born after 1960.

The second trust (RHS) accumulates to $307,500 at age 67, and though not heritable, applies to each individual's post-retirement healthcare security. Over two-thirds of lifetime medical expenses occur after retirement, 28% alone in the last year of life. Unused balances in this trust will transfer to reduction of the National Debt.

In addition, the extra $12 billion dollars annually that will be invested in Lifetime Educational Support (LES) will benefit all citizens immediately.

We have now invested $60 billion annually.

(We have jumped the gun to tell you where *Compound Capitalism* is going. **How we will pay for it with *Big Bills on the Sidewalk* will come later.** The first step of new citizen asset ownership is made formal by citizen ownership of special trust accounts that fund both **Retirement Income Security** and **Retirement Healthcare Security**, the two personal accounts to be fully detailed later.)

Chapter 5. Compound Capitalism, Government and Politics

We have been thinking about a new metaphor to describe an **evolving** United States capitalist government. In a republic favoring democratic capitalism, we imagine the government itself as being a firm, an enterprise—with a CEO and officers (President, Senate and Congress) all elected by the people, and with a board of directors (Supreme Court) overseeing the rights of all.

In the most real sense, we begin the process of being American capitalists at birth, so now is the perfect time for directing adult attention to that idea. We also begin our lives with inherited genetic, emotional and cultural proclivities. We have been waiting for the rational realization of the shareholder part of the American dream to finally become fully hereditary; improving both our tendencies toward cooperation and altruism; rewards in return for participation. The immediate focus, however, is on the gift not yet given; an actual certificate of ownership —a new kind of birth document—a stock option exercised at issue—skin-in-the-game.

An American legacy of freedom already exists, backed by the known asset value of one's future and potential productivity both as a good citizen and as a financial contributor to the goals of American society. Therefore, official recognition of a capital value of our pre-existing assets can be accounted for at birth or adult naturalization.

Since an asset already exists, it is a citizen birthright—and your immediately enhanced lifetime productivity provides new form and substance to the evolving concept of freedom.

Better than just higher taxes on accomplishment, we now have better incentives that promote taxable potential, a better strategy for developing both human accomplishment, real capital assets and government revenues. In an era of advanced technology we must nurture opportunities of the spirit, changing outlooks so that opportunities for education and training will be more fully utilized when available.

So, let me ask you, have you ever considered yourself as a shareholder of your government? Most will answer: *"Not yet."* **Did you ever think of the potential change of status between the words taxpayer and shareholder?** Have you ever thought of the word incentive as having a relationship to opportunity, or reward as being a result of responsibility? Have you thought of your friends as being reflections of yourself, or of them being mirrors of you? Have you ever thought of your parents as being investors in your economic or cultural future, not only through your inherited genes and far beyond having a nose like theirs?

Embracing the Political Third Rail

Throughout *Compound Capitalism*, we will argue that exchanging the word "opportunity" for entitlement will eliminate the not presently embraceable 'third rail of politics,' the *'Unsustainable'* nature of Social Security and post retirement Medicare. The truly democratic and fully energized and embraceable new third rail is that of applied compound interest. Rather than risking one's political career by touching the new third rail, leadership will now discover cheers in its embrace, a true and self-renewing source of energy, the collective power of the people they represent.

This vision of a *'productivity multiplier'* extends an advance tax-credit on improved productivity and good citizenship before its actual arrival. The truth is, the asset value of a good citizen, capitalized early, adds much to whatever potential existed before and it jump-starts the magic of compound interest. In truth, the worth of a motivated citizen is probably much greater than the minimal amount selected. It seems somewhat arbitrary, almost as though we set aside a mere four months income today (under current Social Security projected from birth to age 67) that will be compounded to age 67 into life changing assets.

We didn't ask political leadership for a credit as large as we believe the citizen potential deserves, because, after all, we are trying to *Slay* two specific ***"Unsustainable"*** *Dragons of Debt*, present Social Security and post age 67 Medicare and health costs. To do this, we now have the magic spear of *'Compound interest'* on our side, an economic catalyst of extraordinary power.

This does not suggest that American capitalism has gone weak in the knees, or that options are limited, but that the cultural capitalism that has existed till now is overdue for an intelligent and timely evolutionary redesign, enabling us to profit from trial-by-jury history. It is time for a financial and shareholding facelift. **If the strongest capitalist nation makes a first creative step, chances are good that many nations will be quick to adjust their models positively.**

If capitalism were an evolutionary theory, it would adjust to aid its own survival, not to hasten its extinction. This change of design will help shorten the transition effects from old to new by helping to maintain the expected income of those who depend upon its future delivery. This assists in keeping unbacked promises. They do not have a guaranteed promise now.

We need to have the kind of security that benefits ourselves, but that also benefits the continuation of the institutional enterprise of our government. We find this to be a utilitarian objective. We can best do both by allowing the firm of government to use its revenues to better the firm, while we use our personal human capital assets to better ourselves.

In a democratic *Compound Capitalism* nation, citizens must be converted to actual shareholders and begin thinking of our governing leadership as a firm, an enterprise, both a giant and creative corporation.

What is significant as a starting point in describing small and larger social relationships in America is that we are a *"We"* nation, with a capital letter, not a *'them'* nation. The *"We"* used as our descriptive element implies a unity, self-striving—yes, but individuals assimilated into a larger culture as not only *"I am"* but firmly united in *"We are."*

While America is a conglomeration of races, religions, ethnicities, languages and environments, our new bond of common ownership, belonging and loyalty adds to our culture—and our culture is more than our right to vote—but a right to participate. In viewing *Compound Capitalism* as a philosophy, or even a different form of culture, all would recognize immediately that you can't have unbelievers, particularly the 58% of them who are not present shareholders.

When each new American becomes a citizen, either by birth or naturalization, all that exists now is what we might call *'citizen value,'* an asset of yet untapped and unrealized potential. At the beginning stage, it is not known whether our new Americans will become famous or infamous on life's stage, either a John Quincy Adams or John Wilkes Booth.

In a land of opportunity, that seems just fine. Studies confirm that only a small number are born into financial wealth. In time, however, some means of identification by accomplishment, large or small, will emerge. We know from experience that most of our greatest citizen success stories have roots springing from humble beginnings.

Some people have described that striving phenomenon as *'The American Dream'* whereas others have coined phrases like *'Land of Opportunity.'* However described, we take pride in it. **Our intent is to multiply its power, no matter what we call it, spirit, soul, heart or untapped potential.**

The combined official spirit of all the people, the elected leadership that speaks for us in the broader name of the Constitutional *'We the People,'* understands better than most that the opportunity of individuals, singular, springs from the opportunity of all, plural. Inherently and constitutionally, America believes in potential. We grant rights. And well we might, because faith in the future—confidence—is the spark of progress.

The people combined are the first to realize the potential of people individual, potential expressed for both good and ill. The communal means through which so many recognize this opportunity, democratic government, realizes this best of all. The reason is that individual potential manifests itself by the contributions of all. Those persons who once represented only unknown bundles of energized potential finally begin to make their presence felt. The ongoing pursuit of happiness is expressed in many ways; simple acts that pleasure those dearest to us, heroic acts serving our family, military and nation, and public service acts to total strangers.

Each of us supports the potential of the nation through good works, good citizenship and through the support of financial contributions we call taxes. For a citizen, we think making money for other shareholders is much more emotionally rewarding when she is also one of the shareholders. **If a child can be born as a shareholder of Federal debt, she can also be born as a shareholder in its surplus and success.**

Perhaps in America's earlier days, giving citizens the right to 'homestead' a plot of free ground was the best of 'perks' within the reach of what could be offered to enhance latent individual productivity. Forty acres and a mule. In those early days, there was plenty of land, but few tax revenues (there were no income taxes) with which to enhance productivity, nor were there any insights that better advantaged citizens might one day pay more in taxes. Now we have little land but plenty of taxes, those collected and those existing only in yet unrealized potential.

Watch Out for the Black Swan!

A Black Swan effect is not seeing something that exists. All swans were once believed to be white until their opposite was discovered in Australia. Today, many believe that all that is to be discovered about economics and finance is already known. Economics, particularly the economics of academia, has a blind spot, a inherent deficit for not seeing what's in the rear-view mirror, a Black Swan effect that causes far too many crashes into what's directly on the road ahead. The need for accepting innovative ideas is too often one of uncertainty or denial. New knowledge differs from data in the intellectual constructs that are inferred from it. Productivity has big future economic impacts. **It is also a Black Swan. Why?**

We Need Citizen Productivity Shareholding

We feature a Black Swan in the rear-view mirror, because productivity is measured after-the-fact as a tail-end event. Rather than wait until such unknown events are more volatile, our enterprise will do well not to expose itself to risks of bad guesses, but will prepare for an unknown ability to benefit from future gains in productivity caused by new knowledge.

The future *'Black Swan'* contingency is crucial because of the rapid compounding speed of applied science and technology, that productivity grows faster than wages. The *'Black Swan'* crash in the making is that productivity is flying too high above wages.

What computers, robotics and electronics have brought to the workplace has outpaced wage increases, sometimes vastly so. In order to not have future wage increases tied lock-step into future productivity increases that widen the wage/productivity gap, the ability of citizen shareholders to become an integral part of the longer-term financial engine will shift some of the productivity gains toward wage earners recently merged by their *Compound Capitalism* shareholder interests. Wage earners will now own part of the productivity increases, not just the more advantaged.

This structural balancing is a timely response to allowing workers to share, on their own part, the productivity increase. This will insure that the past owners of the tools of production will not also become the sole future owners and beneficiaries of advancing science and technology. **Workers are now stockholders in the same advances.**

Today, we need neither advanced mathematics degrees nor extraordinary wisdom to grasp the vision that increasing the potential of individuals from birth mightily increases the full potential of the nation.

More Politics

Big Bills Left on the Sidewalk, billions of them! Do we have anyone in Washington to pick them up? Government leaders can now fund RSA, RHA and LES, all improvements at birth for each newborn citizen and every new legally naturalized citizen; and at the same time improve security outlooks for all those present citizens now under Social Security, Medicare and Medicaid. A good society protects all its members from dangers.

As you know, on the 3rd of every month, our government sends out Social Security checks. If a check for a married couple is $1,500, the check costs the government $1,500. They pay today with current 100-cent dollars rather than $1.25 cent dollars. **Which is better?**

But if they paid with dollars that had accumulated for 67 years at 6.5% interest, $1,500 would have cost only 1.25%, or $18.75. It is also your money, citizen's money and government leader's money. Would you and the government rather pay $1500, or would both choose to pay $18.75? And what if even the $18.75 was free? It is.

Arithmetic Still Matters

At the Peterson Foundation fiscal summit in Washington in May of 2011, former President Bill Clinton addressed *"permanent structural deficits,"* saying:

"Arithmetic still matters. We must focus on entitlement spending for the same reason Willie Sutton robbed banks. That's where the money is."

We have very recently spent $800 billion dollars to stimulate the economy, 50 times the proposed yearly *Compound Capitalism* funding. That hasn't worked well, and they were 100-cent dollars, not 1.25 cent compound interest dollars as detailed above.

If arithmetic still matters, can it matter in Washington? How can government add to the national savings rate? What would be a reason why government can't consider 100% discounted dollars to pay for retirement obligations occurring 67 years into the future? **What can government do to have it, give it, and still have it?**

Compound interest is *"where the money is,"* an ideal tool is at hand. And we don't need to rob banks like Willie Sutton, because the *Big Bills* are in plain sight. If government does not address *"permanent structural deficits"* when there is such easy money, what arithmetic lesson still matters? Is no one paying attention in Congress?

If America is to make hard choices and not saddle American children with a debt they cannot pay, why not make the easy choices when the opportunity arises? President Clinton had it right.

"Arithmetic matters even more."

The needed current debt debate between the White House and Congress is far from resolved, each merely having presented trial-balloon budget alternatives, to be resolved, hopefully, soon after the 2016 election. Even current levels of spending, as a percent of GDP, have exceeded tax revenues, having grown from 18.2% of GDP in 2000 to a present average of 24.4%. The increase is 6.2%. Every 1% of GDP is approximately $150 billion dollars, so 6.2% is 6.2 times $150 billion, or $930 billions—almost a trillion dollars.

"A billion here, a billion there; pretty soon you are talking about real money." So said the late Senator Everett Dirksen.

We are currently debating raising the debt ceiling. America has raised the debt ceiling 74 times since 1962, just 49 years, about once every eight months. Restraint, discipline and responsibility are forgotten words. We need a much better direction for argument, one that allows us to start reducing the debt.

Increasing government debt, viewed as compound interest in reverse motion, can be a spear to the heart of any society, because continually increasing a nation's interest on debt, $223 billon of it today, builds the debt payment obligation by leaps and bounds making the financial recovery harder. The spear must be directed against the *Dragon of Debt*, not the institutional enterprise of America. In 2015, the U.S. spent $223 billion, or 6 percent of the federal budget, paying for **interest** on the **debt**. In recent years, **interest rates** have been at historic lows. As they return closer to normal levels, the amount the **government** spends on **interest** will rise.

Rules are important. There are few activities that run smoothly without rules. In the case of financials, certain essential measures for responsible regulation call out for strict adherence. Since citizen's money will be invested, how will that happen and who will watch the money?

To make that first change in capital ownership status legal, permanent and easily recognizable, *Retirement Security Accounts* and *Retirement Healthcare Accounts* are funded by investments in two independently managed investment trusts, most likely indexed funds, with a combined annual investment of $48 billion, $32 billion of that in RSA accounts and $16,000 in RHA accounts ($8,000 and $4,000 each for 4,000,000 the average number of persons born and naturalized yearly) new shareholders. The two trusts will soon become the world's largest and richest portfolios.

Accordingly and importantly: We are not advocates of government directly investing in private markets. Investment should be managed by experts on behalf of government.

Preventing both influence and politics to corrupt bureaucrats and elected officials should be a built-in restrictive priority. We must be wary, given the past record of government investing, both in the U.S. and abroad.

Past Federal Reserve Chairman Alan Greenspan gave the same precautionary advice:

"I don't know of any way you can essentially insulate government decision-makers from having access to what will amount to very large investments in American private industry … I have been around long enough to realize that that is just not credible and not possible. Somewhere along the line, that breach will be broken."

Mr. Greenspan was thinking, we believe, of the usual suspects, the descriptive words like *'influence peddling,'* *'theft,' 'bribery,' 'extortion,' 'corruption,' 'nepotism' and 'cronyism.'* We favor built-in safeguards, an anti-tampering design, fail-safe and adult-proof.

It is important to acknowledge that allowing the government to directly invest funds in private markets might distort the free-market system or politicize the process of investment. Therefore, that route of privatization is not considered here. We have tended to favor SEC oversight of authorized non-government professional investment firms, perhaps carefully selected consortiums of experts, perhaps also with additional regulatory oversight.

We anticipate that large consortiums of investment experts, rather than individual investment and/or advisory firms, would handle what would soon become the world's largest investment trusts. We would anticipate that the investment vehicles might well be index funds rather than investments dominated by only the largest corporations. (We will suggest later that in exchange for significantly reduced Federal Corporate Tax rates, that all present and future U.S. corporate entities contribute 2% of their stock, voting and non-voting, as their tax-reduction carrot.)

According to *The Wall Street Journal,* the S&P 500 had a 9.1% return over the last 20 years. We favor investment trusts which have pre-set structural guidelines to establish the portfolio balance of investments that will be included. These balance rules would be allowed sufficient flexibility to react to market swings, but also flexibility tempered by cautious and constant regulatory oversight. Value investing and market capitalization methods might be mixed together.

To prevent politics from doing its worst, *Compound Capitalism* argues for a requirement that no greater than 4% of funds may be invested in government securities. (That is because of the government's 4% interest in the RSA trust.) This is sure to be a subject for debate. There is much evidence to support this caution. Brink Lindsay, again in *Against the Dead Hand,* advises that:

"… Government meddling in how private accounts are to be invested can reduce returns for investors, often catastrophically."

He goes on to cite how investing excessively in government securities risks turning investments into *"dumping grounds for government debt."* Moreover, he suggests that governments are immune from desirable competitive pressure to earn decent returns and often prone to invest in ways that are politically advantageous, but economically suspect.

Accordingly, the Cato Project and other privatization proponents agree on the role of government in investment based pension plans. Cato Institute put it this way:

"Allowing the federal government to purchase stocks would give it the ability to obtain a significant, if not a controlling interest in virtually every major company in America. Experience has shown that even a two to three percent block of shares can give an activist shareholder substantial influence over the policies of publicly traded companies. The result could be a government bureaucrat sitting on every corporate board, a grim prospect that builds few advocates for government investing."

The risk of retiring without income has been in a desperate race with having reduced income in the present. As Brink Lindsay again puts it:

"… Substituting political risk for market risk has been a poor bargain indeed, as governments have been forced to renege on promises and slash benefits to stave off financial collapse."

Highly experienced professionals, well aware of the needs for balanced risk and safety, manage most pension plans. What seems to hold true is that funds managed by skilled professionals over long periods of time have tended to even out and account for the cycles of markets, interest rates and economic growth patterns. Over the long haul, returns have been predictable.

Although invested monies could be poorly managed, chances are much better that they will be reasonably well managed. There are many successful investment trusts and pension plans. There is proof. Evidence should trump opinion. Even more supportive are the actual results of large, well-managed pensions whose investment histories are known. Generally, large pension funds are known for their stable performance. Hundreds of college and university plans, for example, have been successfully managed. Most larger companies, some employing over 100,000 persons, from IBM to Coca Cola, from Proctor and Gamble to Pfizer have well respected plans, fully diversified. There are thousands of successful pensions among the 10,000 or so publicly traded companies.

The Social Security Trustees themselves have stated that a 6.5% investment return is probable to the stated timeline. That is how we chose that percentage. We previously mentioned that the S&P 500 Index Fund has returned 9.1% over the last 20 years, despite recent lower interest rates.

To maximize account safety, private fund custodians, like mutual fund or pension plan managers, would provide restricted investment fund options designed to limit investment risk (like most large corporate pension plans), but with the regulatory oversight (not government control or input to investment decisions) of the SEC. (Securities and Exchange Commission).

This most important rule is intended to limit the role of government in the purchase and management of assets, while at the same time granting, through the SEC and other government agencies, certain regulatory and oversight responsibilities.

American democratic capitalists believe in capitalism. A fact of life often ignored by Congressional legislators is that capitalism pays the salary of every elected official, their salary—every cent! There is no other *"ism"* upon which American candidates run for elective office. Each Congressman has put their eggs wholly in the basket of free-market democratic capitalism. Therefore, when any one of them shouts demagogic slogans to describe any investment funded proposal for reasoned retirement security, it is a direct repudiation of the very economic system that grants their own running for office and receiving their own very generous pensions, including their own investment funded benefits.

Since the Federal government depends solely upon the success of the capital market for its own money, *Compound Capitalism* seems conceptually well within desirable risk boundaries. If government can depend on capitalism, so indeed can its formal pension plan. **We do and we should have our eggs in the *"democratic capitalism"* basket. This is America.**

We have no tolerance whatsoever in making *'risky investment'* a component of our retirement security system, not that any equity, no matter how solid, is risk free. In the past, however, this accusation has become a knee-jerk reaction to investment based systems, **even though all the ships christened PAYGO have already sunk or are being abandoned worldwide.** The fact is, unless one intends to continue the failed voyage of a sinking ship, the only alternative is an investment-based pension system.

It bears noting that any changes to assumptions will have an equal effect on both PAYGO assumptions and investment-based assumptions. Both influence anticipated income and neither assumption is immune to the variations in economic growth. This is why it is important to look at past assumptions and results over long periods of time.

Both poverty and wealth are heritable. One can leave heirs as consistently poor over several generations as they are presently. (And they tend to do just that. The average person has very little savings to call on.) A better choice can create wealth and leave heirs better off. Given the choice between these options, who among us, all other things being equal, would put their dollar into a poorly managed government bureaucracy rather than a professionally managed pension program?

There are excellent pension programs, but there are no successful PAYGO systems. The latter have never worked. Therefore, calling reasoned pension management *"privatization"* tends to rob it of its historical status.

Such anti-capitalist rhetoric to describe well-accepted corporate institutions is shameful. Privatization carries the false connotation that *"something good is being taken away from a previously entitled owner."* Let it be remembered that government can claim no previous ownership to a successful retirement security plan. The only claimants to pension plan success are in the private sector. Pension plans have been around for almost a century; the best of them are both privatized and diversified. It still makes sense.

In richer countries, including America, welfare systems have been held together by political duct-tape, including making income taxable for higher income retirees, skipping inflation indexing temporarily and/or raising the retirement age. In the U.S., the age has now been raised to from 62 to 65, to 67 and 70 is on the table.

Traditionalists are often monarchists at heart, elites envisioning the governing institution itself as supreme ruler, not having accepted the modern concept of customers (market demand) being in command of the enterprise. Such thinking can become a negative force that would prevent the citizens from nurturing independence, of taking command. **Such thinking can keep dependency enthroned and government the core source of benefits for which we are both indebted and indentured. It's a bad model for either mature citizens or an enlightened leadership.**

Perhaps some will not see that as an open-minded criticism even now, but they should, because the *Compound Capitalism* detailed in this book should appeal to those of any political persuasion, as it distributes its form of economic justice as equal opportunity and ownership to all citizens. **Compounding interests is both an impartial, bipartisan and democratic concept. It's a bandwagon political leaders can ride.**

At least some can. Others say: *"Why shouldn't we raise payroll taxes?"* The slogan seems to be: *"Let no smart man mess with a bad thing!"* What is revealing is the ease with which this Chinese water torture of insidious theft continues and is justified politically. The essence of any or most of the so-called reform solutions is that each one confirms another promise broken, not a promise kept. If we expect the newborn to assume the future liabilities of Social Security retirees, before they can even vote to influence their fate, wouldn't it be more in the interest of social justice if we accorded them the minimal courtesy of fair treatment?

There are those, including some in Congress, who claim a rich nation should be able to take as much as it needs from the incomes of its citizens, that tax-collection has the force of law behind it. Some maintain that government, so long as it has the power of law supporting legislative action, can require whatever amounts are needed through taxation. They don't say whether or not one should care if citizens are complacent or belligerent. But this kind of coercive force does not differ much from the tough schoolyard bully, and the intimidating threat of, *"Me and Knuckles are gonna' getcha!"*

We have a situation that is akin to demanding organ transplants from the young and healthy to sustain the old and dying. It is as if someone richer and more powerful claims a right to pull a child from her bike; to seize a kidney at any stop sign, because the older organ candidate is unwilling to await the rare fatal bicycle crash. Perhaps it's not quite that bad, of course, but theft, no matter what is taken, is morally unacceptable.

Past Chairman Alan Greenspan—continued:

"… The spending on the elderly dwarfs what we spend on each child, to some extent, at least, read investment. As a result, the benefits to seniors in America have come increasingly to

dominate the budget ... The elderly-to-child spending ratio in America is higher than in any other industrial country. Second, this comes at a time when in America we have three times as many children as elderly in poverty."

Each new legislative patch-job has represented either a tax increase and/or a reduction of citizen expected benefits. Granted, it was more from the unanticipated architectural faults within the system's structure than by any intended ill-will of political elites that motivated subsequent violations of the promise, but a promise broken is a promise broken, no matter who implemented it or how it is later rationalized.

Unrepentant supporters, by freely giving their continuing support, philosophically integrate the faults of the system within themselves. By doing so, they buy personal ownership of a bad thing, transforming faults of the supported idea into faults of the soul. Support of the morally indefensible, slowly over time, forfeits one's ability to disclaim responsibility for their actions. The ill-will not originally intended—deprives its unwary new owners of any moral high ground.

Linguistic demagogues are the suicide terrorists of modern politics. Because of them, proponents of rational *Compound Capitalism* will first need to be aware (and careful) not to lose sight of the fact that even significant basic changes in systems need not be seen as revolutionary, but as natural and rational evolutionary progressions, however broad the reforms may be in scope. **Any time the pie is cut differently is a time ripe for demagogues.** Always at the forefront is the claim that when someone gains, someone else loses—a false and destructive *'zero-sum'* premise.

Despite accusations of deals behind closed doors, it is also both unfair and unreasonable to think that politicians are unmindful of self-interested virtue, or that successful appeals, that are moral, cannot be made that satisfy both pragmatic needs and responsibilities.

Compound Capitalism is trying to do that. In this sense, we have reason to place great hopes in politicians acting wisely in their own self-interests and for the betterment of others.

Acting wisely? **Wise and wizard are not always the same.** If you remember the film, *The Wizard of Oz,* the wizard is revealed to be a mere manipulative man, but he redeems himself, proving to be wise in his handling of the issues put before him. He comes through in the end, not as a wizard, but as a man. We have the same high hopes for our policymakers. When the cowardly lion approached the wizard requesting courage, the wizard could just as well have said, *"It doesn't take courage not to be stupid—it only takes not being stupid."* Who wouldn't prefer the security our leaders have given themselves? Few decline.

Members of Congress who were first elected in 1984 or later are covered by the Federal Employees' Retirement System unless they decline this coverage, in which case they are covered only by Social Security. FERS is composed of three elements:

- Social Security
- The FERS basic annuity, a monthly pension based on years of service and the average of the three highest consecutive years of basic pay.
- The Thrift Savings Plan (TSP), into which participants can deposit up to a maximum of $15,500 in 2007. Their

employing agency matches employee contributions up to 5% of pay.

Few decline their much better than average citizen options. What about the rest of us?

We need *Compound Capitalism* listeners in Washington leadership. Most economists speak with one voice, that deficits crowd out productive investment, vacuuming up potential savings and raising, after inflation, interest rates. When national security has to compete with retirement and health security, it does not make for easy decision making. Security is a continuing threat—just look at the daily news. And the *'defense budget'* defends not just territory, but everything we hold dear in our lives.

Foreseeing future disturbances, none will be more threatening than those that divert or destroy, in significant magnitude, scarce economic resources. These resources are sorely needed, now more than ever, to maintain the prosperity, safety and leadership role of the enterprise. The world stage is already set for further such disruptions throughout the Middle East, North Africa and Sub-Saharan Africa, Latin America, North Korea and even China.

The (DoD) 2018 Defense budget request is for $715 billion dollars. Defending a nation's internal economic future is also a strategic defense posture, as a nation unable to defend its banks or medical needs or repair its highways needs is as weak as a nation unable to pay to defend itself otherwise. You can print money, of course, but it must continue to be worth something.

Compound Capitalism's big three, RSA, RHA and LES calls for only $60 billion, 8.5% of the DoD budget, not

$715 billion. That's a fantastic defending of America bargain.

And if you are truly imaginative, think about how the main business, America, will have maintained its vision and place in that future. Think about how maintaining the business of security is threatened when over half of the present dollar income is consumed just to support a failing social insurances division, the not so *'invisible hand'* is picking the pocket of the institutional enterprise. What will it take for strong national security to survive in the future?

As with any other world-changing era, an age of technology requires great faith in the future. This faith will not be easily found or maintained if we squander our future economic resources in paying for what we already know to be a failed experience. Expecting too little of markets is just as irrational as expecting too much. New technology is the future. **Perhaps the truly *'irrational exuberance'* is thinking that failed systems will somehow take care of themselves in the future. The future will come, whether we try to postpone it or not.**

Foreign nations hold half of our assets. Dividends and interest are paid to foreigners who hold those assets. The U.S. dollar has been the world currency of choice. That selfish interest matters, because given a choice, most nations would prefer having their own citizens receive returns, rather than the nationals of other nations. Low interest rates tend to drive the value of the dollar down and destroy the value of bonds. Closest to America in the capitalist West are those sharing a similar economic past and a common language. Those same nations face the problem of increasing deficits and aging populations. **We think the *Compound Capitalism* model has legs.**

We must first demand that our leaders lead. Politicians want to influence us and they should, but we must also learn how to influence them. Only when they understand that opportunity for *'life, liberty and the pursuit of happiness'* requires that these virtues must grow and be more widely shared, will we make our voices heard. For now, those virtues are more and more restricted.

Can Political Leadership Listen?

We believe they can.

Another Nobel Laureate in economics is James Buchanan. With Gordon Tullock, he wrote *The Calculus of Consent: Logical Foundations of Constitutional Democracy.* In it, the authors make a reasoned case as to why the potential of the political process is both underused and misused. Nonetheless, it is a hopeful scenario.

To begin, he says: *"The central notion of mutuality of gain may be carried over to the political relationship." That "… the only test for the mutuality of gain is agreement." and that: "… mutuality of gain can occur among all members of a group."*

In discussing differences between what is and what ought to be, Buchanan believes the citizens (and other politicians) would be much better off by remembering what brings people together as humans rather than what separates them as politicians. He suggests that each one of us is a *"rational utility maximizing,"* being.

He, too, suggests, like Adam Smith, that the politician acts in his/her self-interest, but certainly among those self interests are those he shares with his constituents. There is no issue of right or wrong implied in that. He believes that the political process (collective action) is a cooperative action in which all parties, conceptually, stand to gain. This is opposed to the zero-sum claim that one's gain is another's loss.

He says the idea of trade for mutual benefit is a cornerstone of exchange relationships and that a bargaining range exists in determining fair shares. Such persons, confronted with choices between fair sharing and fraudulent behavior opt for the former. Certainly, each person has individual moral standards and we value their standards most by the range of freedom given to express them. In the case of public persons, there are external costs imposed by those expressions.

If there is any lesson in this, it seems that more successful bargaining might be made by appealing to the logic and values of individuals rather than groups, and to constituent groups rather than to party affiliation groups.

Like Buchanan, we share a faith that man can rationally organize his own society and that nothing in the social order is exempt from rational choice.

Hopefully, both reason and passion will converge in suggesting an appropriate means of building and strengthening social relationships. There is nothing in either reason or passion that makes the present system compulsive. An economic approach suggests that one spend his political capital wisely and that approaches containing appeals to justice have strong relevance in democratic societies, not just our own.

The politician and the citizen live in the same society. To do so successfully, one must not exploit or restrict the freedom of another through the imposition of either bad policies or bad citizenship.

This rule of common sense, we believe, supports the idea that pursuit of private gain can be put in the most advantageous forms for widespread social use. What can be achieved has much stronger appeal. When individuals act collectively for retirement security and educational goals, it should be the objective that the customers like the result just as much as it should be the aim of *Friskies* that the cats like the cat food. Why should anyone settle for less?

As Buchanan suggests further: *"The State must be considered merely as a device, not as an end in itself. A State does not have either preferences or aversions and feels no pleasure or pain."* Buchanan agreed that Samuelson was correct in pointing out, that *"citizens agree to the establishment of the State because it provides the means of providing services needed by all."*

Concluding the discussion, Buchanan and Tullock agree that the State should not have a monopoly of force, that we should do everything possible to avoid the State with too much power.

"The State should have enough power to keep the peace, but not enough to provide temptation to ambitious men. The State should never be given enough power to prevent genuinely popular uprisings against it."

We are trying to maintain focus on what to do tomorrow, not what we did yesterday.

The Arithmetic Lesson In Review

(Feb 9, 2018) It's still tax day. $20,627,304,557,400 is today's debt. The national debt is on the front page of every

day's paper. That's trillions first and then billions, and growing.

Legislators did figure out along the way some of what they had overlooked regarding life expectancy, rates of birth and needs for income. But not fully, as we are living much longer. What has happened is that there have been many changes to the present system, the most obvious of which are that payroll taxes have had to increase steadily and that retirement ages have had to be bumped ahead—first from an early 62 option to 65, now to 67 and with age 70 now under serious consideration. For most of the people who pay no income taxes, their payroll tax is the biggest tax obligation, and it is withdrawn from every earner's paycheck, with an equal contribution from the employer.

These rates apply to earnings up to the maximum ($106,800) taxable amount.

The Tax Relief, Unemployment Insurance Reauthorization and Job Creation Act of 2010 reduced 2011 Social Security tax rates for employees and self-employed people by two percentage points, from 6.2 percent to 4.2 percent for employees and from 12.4 percent to 10.4 percent for self-employed people.

These tax rates have returned to 6.2% and 12.4%, so let's stick with that for the moment. We are better informed keeping the $106,800 figure in mind. Therefore, for a person earning only a third of maximum, $32,072, the tax to the employee at 6.2% is $1,988 annually. At $50,000, 6.2% is $3,100. At maximum it is $6,622. Both require equal employer taxes.

It is an assumption throughout *Compound Capitalism* that new savings, other *Big Bills* gained by finding solutions to problems that are presently unsolved, will be considered as *'found money'* savings by government officials and others, and that those gains will be have required debt reduction **preferences** over new spending priorities.

Our preference is that legislators would be prohibited from discretionary spending allocations of pre-identified *Big Bills on the Sidewalk* savings, excepting national security, until the present $19+ trillion in National Debt is retired. **This strengthens the dollar as a world currency, which is also important.**

All prior and present tax and other citizen contributions have already paid for the transformation in in allowing the meaning of the word *'capitalist'* to expand both the shareholder membership rolls and citizenship roles for every American. What is intended is for all present and future U.S. citizens to be henceforth considered as full shareholders in the enterprise of America, and that prior yet unrecognized capital investments have already paid the price of future stakeholder membership dues.

Nothing is more personal than affection. To begin, since we can't tell people we love them enough times, we can set the forces in motion that speak those words in our absence, and perhaps much better by deed than we might try to say it. Now that you know that your grandchildren will be financially secure at retirement age, and with money to pass on to the heirs you may never meet, it is time to address a topic we will revisit, the how to concept of compounding capitalism as well as interests, financial and personal.

Albert Einstein's advice that compound interest is *"the greatest miracle ever discovered,"* is also our best chance to *'stand on the shoulders of a giant.'*

Chapter 6. Slaying the First Dragon of Debt: Social Security

Slaying the Dragon of Debt: The Spear of Compound Capitalism.

We now attack the *Dragon of Debt* in single file, one spear thrust at a time, starting with Social Security, (a Pay-As You-Go, PAYGO system).

Author Brink Lindsey, in his insightful book, *Against the Dead Hand: The Uncertain Struggle for Global Capitalism*, details the PAYGO failings in nation after nation, from Uruguay and Brazil to Belgium and the former Soviet empire.

All nations have failed to address the crisis of demographics. In Venezuela, the average pension dropped 80% in less than twenty years due to inflation. In Argentina, in the seven years between a 1985 and 1992, the loss was 30%. Others merely made drastic benefit cuts to stop the bleeding. By the mid-1990's, contribution rates ranging from 26% in the Czech Republic to 30.5% in Hungary and 42% in Bulgaria had crushed incentive!

The first U.S. inherited characteristic we will change is the heritable and *'unsustainable'* weakness of our own Social Security System. To start that process, think Retirement Security Accounts instead. We will begin now to separate overlapping and duplicative concepts. For example, we will separate 'disability' from retirement, because it is different from retirement and from Retirement Healthcare Security, which is different as well.

A *Compound Capitalism* productivity tax-credit granted now represents a one-time credit and a "lifetime benefit." The $8,000 investment to control future debt will be made toward Retirement Security Accounts. Invested at new births and new citizen naturalizations today, it compounds at age 67 to $615,000. Final accounts for naturalized citizens will have less years earning growth, and will thus be less in total at 67. (6.5% interest is deemed conservative by the Social Security Trustees.)

The $8,000 granted at birth (or citizenship) totals only a tiny four months retirement income at age 67 as anticipated under current Social Security projected to 2083, 67 years hence.

When anyone knows well in advance, a government for example, that they have certain known liabilities that will occur far in the future, the stage is perfectly set to cover those obligations with funds that cost 1.25 cents on the dollar rather than choosing to pay in current dollars that cost 100 cents each. The savings is 98.75%. It's a no brainer!

Why would anyone choose to pay 100 cents on each dollar when they could use compound interest and pay only 1.25 cents on the dollar? You should care about this because it is your money. That's what $77 dollars for every dollar invested means. Why not exchange those particular dollars into common sense?

Using discounted dollars on the largest government future expenditures also enables legislators to have many more flexible options in solving the long-term health insurance risks of those already born and naturalized, whether the choices made are for full healthcare, major medical support, insurance vouchers or some other proposal under consideration to cover interim and non-retirement years.

Whatever the choice, the term 'unsustainable' gets a solid chance for a more attractive name change because we first solve longer-term issues.

Compound Interest Chart at 6.3%, 6.5%, 6.8% and 7.3%

Account Holder's Invested Value

Effects of Compounding Interest on Initial Investment of $8,000

Year	Interest Rate			
	6.30%	6.50%	6.80%	7.30%
10	$15,885	$16,234	$16,771	$17,707
20	29,777	31,043	33,041	36,662
30	55,818	59,359	65,094	75,908
40	104,632	113,506	128,242	157,167
50	196,134	217,043	252,648	325,413
60	367,657	415,027	497,740	673,767
67	538,830	615,657	751,884	1,049,034

If the average person lived to age 67 and before one cent of income as interest on the principle was spent, then 268 million recipients, each living to age 67, would receive a cumulative total of $615,000 times 268 million accounts.

At not one cent of net cost to the U.S. government enterprise, the total return to that multiplication is $164.820 trillion dollars. That's one hundred sixty-four trillion, eight hundred-twenty billion dollars!

That is approximately 82 times our present $20 trillion GDP. That is *Compound Capitalism*.

Each of the annual estimated 4,000,000 new individual **Retirement Security Accounts** is a U.S. shareholder investment of $8,000, and is equal for both males and females, **mending a long-term gender bias.**

In startling comparison to Social Security, PAYGO (Pay-As-You-Go), the citizen shareholder productivity tax credit at birth solves for all time the total retirement security portion of the Retirement Security Account!

Interest at 6.5% on the principal and compounding interest would provide $40,008 annually or $3,334 monthly, all without reducing the principal inheritable by one's heirs. (Totals from grants at citizen naturalization would be smaller, not having started at birth)

It should be shouted from the rooftops that a retired husband and wife would enjoy a joint annual retirement income of $80,016, since each retiree has his/her own account. Concurrently, each retired husband/wife combination has also created inheritable wealth of $1,231,314! This plan eliminates the flawed and unsustainable long-term deficit portion of the currently unfunded Social Security future. The return is approximately $77 for every initial $1 invested.

(In addition, each individual has $307,500 in a Retirement Healthcare Account or another $615,000 for a couple. Retirement Healthcare Accounts help to protect the heritable assets of family estates, not just one's health. **RHS is detailed later.**)

Transition Costs

A transition is a changeover to a new financing source, not a retreat from prior commitments! To the extent that needed money is borrowed, future generations will have an interest cost added on top of whatever the transition costs will be. We must avoid borrowed money.

Because of the out-of-control growth of Medicare and Medicaid, *Compound Capitalism* asks that all major social benefits in the future be funded and managed as separate programs and accounting items—rather than being lumped together, a confusing jumble of bookkeeping entries that like 'Fibber McGee's closet,' make efficient cost management difficult and accountability impossible. It would separate SSI, DI, Medicare and Medicaid into independent pre-age 67 social insurance programs, so that potential accounting and administrative shortcomings can be addressed in a more competent manner.

Only part of this delicious lunch is free. That's because the unfunded obligations of prior invitations must be met. One way or another, the transition costs to a new system will be paid for. Are there ways in which those in the current system are also invited to lunch?

The answer is yes. Fixing some problems often entails a willingness to start again from scratch, otherwise promises of the past are lost and hope for the future is denied. *Compound Capitalism* allows for promises already made to be kept, a major benefit. That this small part of the vast reserve of our future productivity be advanced to us as a guaranteed solution to the shackles prior leadership has placed upon us allows us to insist that future Americans be set free, emancipated from the chains of the present system they have endured.

Therefore, we anticipate defining all those already born, but not yet retired, as *'transitional persons.'* All of these persons are already in the current system and in its accounting. Until *Compound Capitalism* is enacted, some will continue to be classed as 'transitional persons' between 0 and 67. Most of the *'transitional persons'* are now working.

One might fairly say that the constant need for *'make-up'* money to keep social programs afloat is a systemic risk defect that would be regarded as a loss of principal in an ordinary investment. Therefore, based on the number of past *'make-ups'* (calls on margin) that have been necessary, (changes in payroll taxes and retirement ages) have all clearly defined a risky investment.

These many calls on margin, in the overview, contribute to present Social Security being classed as a poor investment when one compares the money invested in Social Security against the return-on-investment from private pension fund investments. Private investment, in this comparison, wins—hands down!

Moreover, when you recall that the 'make-ups' keep only the promises to the recipients, but break all promises to those who pay, then the weighty defect of moral hazard tips any scale of balance and ends any comparative doubt.

And that's not the worst of it. Don't fail to consider the moral risk of bad promises. To date, there has been nothing to prevent government from making promises it couldn't (and didn't) keep. And they weren't promises to begin with because there were no guarantees. Broken promises of that ilk by government weaken citizen faith in and respect for political institutions. This is the ultimate unacceptable moral risk to a democratic republic.

People were promised lesser taxes, earlier retirement ages, etc. Those promises were not kept. Without breaking current expectations, future benefits will not be delivered at the so-called promised costs or ages. The fault is not in the intent, but the nature of the promise. One can't promise future birth and death rates due to the great advances in science and medicine.

Government may ask who benefits most from such a creative reform. We list government itself as the primary beneficiary, as the cost for sustaining Retirement Security Accounts and Retirement Healthcare Accounts after 2083 (when those born tomorrow start to retire) would drop to $0 billions annually, an incredible savings. And that doesn't count any savings represented by interest paid on national debt.

After 67 years, all future Retirement Security Account holders and all Retirement Healthcare Account holders will pay $0, as they have held benefits from birth or naturalization.

The next biggest savings are realized by business and corporate America. After transitional costs are met, (67 years hence) corporate America saves half of the Social Security payroll withholding tax, allowing greater wages, more internal investment and/or greater profits.

After 67 years have passed, all citizens will be enrolled in the new system: *Compound Capitalism.*

In any event, and in the meantime, all those persons who fall within the *'transitional'* definition would have their pension benefits guaranteed at the rate they would have received had the present Social Security system continued to their retirement age. These safeguards are needed so that promises made become promises kept.

We must structurally eliminate *'moral hazard.'*

What is *'moral hazard?'* to the account holder? In the same spirit of prudence, permitting account holders to invest their account funds on their own before having met the *'moral hazard'* requirements of being able to guarantee a minimum retirement income for themselves is not responsible. It puts both their fellow citizens and their government at risk by failing to account for individual financial shortcomings, bad luck or irresponsibility.

A well-designed system must answer the irresponsibility issue by its structure. We may look the other way when citizens fail other obligations, but we must not allow this pension system to fail due to bad planning, or to fail the means test of eliminating *'moral hazard.'*

Since each person would have a personal account, there would be no need to make special provisions regarding divorce or spousal relationships. After one generation of this program, of course, all future citizens would have individual accounts. Future spouses would have accounts independent of the other spouse, children have accounts independent of parents and other siblings. Therefore, there is no need to have special spousal benefits related to the premature death of an account holder, as all premature deaths trigger predetermined vested deposits to be returned to heirs. **(Study the scale of asset vesting detailed in this book's Appendix)**

We prefer a system producing inheritable wealth and both pension and retirement health benefits over a system producing only promises of benefits and no wealth. Given that choice, why not produce wealth that can be left to heirs? This is both the moral option and the moral question.

Anyone professing any reasoned concern for the poor or less well off should be the first to favor the widespread growth of inheritable wealth. There is no moral high ground in opposing this predictable consequence. From a moral view, according to Daniel Shapiro of the West Virginia University Philosophy Department, *"it (an individualized retirement pension account) is fairer, provides more freedom to run our lives, provides more security and creates less antagonism between generations, fostering a greater sense of community."*

Egalitarians, who favor fairness as a key aspect of social justice, can't find fault with the balanced nature of this form of an equal head start at birth. None can assure that all will end equally, nor should they. All organisms are different and we favor this as a form of free will. Chosen mutual advantage is far more positive than certain inequality. Cooperation is the more morally balanced of birthrights.

We firmly believe that one measure a great nation must sustain is a system that provides a bedrock of retirement security upon which further wealth can be built.

The public does have money for social purposes, but not an unlimited money supply for everyone's special utopian entitlement. We are born with differences. Our position accepts that there are constant trade-offs in life in which one better good must often be chosen in lieu of another good. There is no special-interest, full-service cornucopia of 'make a wish' welfare. This is an entitlement of skin-in-the-game shareholder citizenship.

We have covered the need to avoid the *'moral hazard'* of allowing a structural flaw that would permit any account holder to squander the retirement security portion of his/

her account through willing or unwitting acts. By the same token, the enterprise—the institution of government must also be protected against structural defect. A sliding scale of asset value settled in the primary account is designed to protect the grantor (government) against lost citizenship value by reason of premature death of the account holder. **(See Appendix for the Account Holder's Vested Value Table.)**

It is obvious, when studying the value table in the Appendix that we have recognized the fact that the productivity assumed in granting a future productivity tax credit does not occur all at once. People are productive over long periods of time. Until they have fully earned what they have been rewarded for in advance, it does not yet fully accrue to them. The investment must be protected. We have said that accounts vest to the account holder incrementally, which the table shows. What it also shows is that the account holder owns 49% of the account at age 20, but 96% of the account is vested in favor of the account holder at age 67 and beyond.

At an account holder's age 43, for example, a deceased's estate would receive 72% of an account valued at $129,917, or $93,540. This is in stark contrast to present Social Security paying nothing. In this example, $36,377 would be returned to what we have called the Debt Reduction Trust. This vesting system acknowledges that the tax-credit grantor (our government) has suffered a productivity loss by the premature loss of the citizen account holder.

How the difference between the asset amount vested and the individualized account value can transfer to the Debt Reduction Trust (at death of an account holder) is clearly shown. If death is prior to age 19, all asset values of the account (Retirement Security Account) transfer to the Debt Reduction Trust.

Please reflect on the amount of funds that would become available by reason of death of account holders before full vesting occurs. You will quickly note that before age 67, each year's separate class of approximately 4,000,000 new entrants creates over $26 billion in RSA mortality revenue.

(In addition RHS accounts return all accumulated funds to the Debt Reduction Trust when account holder deaths occur before age 67. RHS funds are for post 67 healthcare.)

The table reflects only raw numbers, not the potential accumulated values should these and other class year's mortality revenues also be invested by government at the baseline 6.5%. This, of course, would make the mortality funds (those funds which return to the system by reason of the premature death of the account holder) much larger, a note for astute policymakers and statisticians to ponder in depth. One might easily speculate that these funds invested at 6.5% might well make the entire proposed debt reduction solution self-perpetuating long before the first 67-year cycle is complete. Our preference is for mortality created returns to reduce the national debt until in no longer exists. Please note, in addition, that the future birth rates are projected to fall, reducing the actuarial funding liability. In other words, the system itself could become entirely self-funded (earning over $48 billion annually) due to the revenues generated by premature deaths, the return of non-vested portions of Retirement Security Accounts and full Retirement Healthcare Accounts of prematurely deceased persons into the system.

(Regarding Retirement Healthcare Accounts, note again that all invested funds are indeed returned to the Debt

Reduction Trust on the occasion of the premature passing of an account holder. The $307,500 in the account accrued to age 67 is exclusively for the healthcare of the living account holder after age 67.)

We suggest that proceeds redeemed through premature death of account holders be immediately used only to reduce debt until Federal debt is retired.

So long as nothing is accomplished by Congress, the debt numbers will only become larger, if one can imagine a number so large. It's the old *"pay me now, or pay me later"* situation where those whose concern is only the next election routinely chose the *"pay me later"* option. The system has made promises and the only way to keep them is to pay, not to say: *"We want either to pay you less, start you later, or charge more—or all of these."* What too many others have been calling 'reforms' are merely sugarcoated ways of being AWOL on promises.

Currently the debate is focused between debt ceilings, future Obama Care, the Ryan Plan and future budgeting issues. *Big Bills* doesn't seem to have entered the talks. Until now, no set of advocates knows about *Compound Capitalism's* rescue lifebuoy—they are too busy trying to repair a sinking lifeboat rather than starting over. The Ryan Plan entertains paying retirees up to $15,000 annually to cover healthcare costs, $3,000 more in a single year than Compound Capitalism requires in a lifetime. We can do much better.

Both President Obama and Congress seemed locked in partisan debate over the future of the present retirement and healthcare systems and the permissible limits on Federal debt.

Within the transitional group of ages 0-67 are massive numbers of presently uninsured. This is just one unresolved problem. There are as many as 50 million citizens who at some time during a year have no insurance coverage. Some think because they are young, they can take a chance by saving the required premium. Others are poor or have lower incomes and are unable to afford expensive coverage. Those who are insured often overuse their benefits. A result of overuse of expensive services may contribute directly to the fact that health costs are increasing at double the rate of the cost-of-living. We read just yesterday that tissue and body parts may soon be printed on 3-D printers. That's good! What else might be in the future?

Although the Social Security, Medicare/Medicaid system has evolved into an income security system rather than the retirement assistance program President Franklin Roosevelt first declared it to be, it is impossible to measure what premiums should be to insure for what has subsequently become covered. As previously stated, DI (Disability Income), SSI (Supplemental Survivor's Insurance), healthcare (Medicare and Medicaid), and employment security benefits should be paid for separately utilizing rigorous actuarial accounting.

Compound Capitalism will considerably broaden the political and economic options for handling the transition period. With long-term retirement income and healthcare security now funded, political debate can more productively engage its energies toward what seems to us to be the crucial next 23 years, until those born tomorrow have begun contributing to payroll taxes. It's the ideal platform for true bipartisan political compromise.

And since something monumental can be done, Congress should actively find a way to smooth the transition from the present systems to *Compound Capitalism*.

Congressional actions might include a revision of the tax system to a VAT or consumption-based system, a reduction in the globally uncompetitive corporate tax rate, and extensive elimination of write-offs. We must design new duplication oversight and accounting methodologies to incorporate sources of savings income into the process of debt reduction, both State and Federal. (See the example of California in the Appendix.)

If the present $19+ trillion in national debt can be substantially reduced or eliminated in the next generation, (we have detailed various means for accomplishing this throughout this book, particularly in the chapters titled *Big Bills on the Sidewalk* and *Other Big Bills on the Sidewalk*), then fresh options to handle the transition period will also compound. *Other Big Bills Left on the Sidewalk* will cover as much as $2 Trillion in annual potential savings that are currently left on other sidewalks.

Age 67 as a retirement age is well into the future as is our knowledge that two-thirds of our life's medical expenses will occur after retirement. Is there any one among us who wouldn't choose to discount their biggest debts?

(A more detailed history of our vulnerable Social Security program is found in the Appendix.)

Chapter 7. Slaying the Second Dragon of Debt: Retirement Healthcare Security

It's still tax day. April 15, 2016 has already passed and we are $19+ trillions in the hole—and the debt clock is ticking louder and louder. It's become an alarm-clock! When we awaken from our role imagining ourselves as political leaders, parents, expectant grandparents or immigrant hopefuls, and act our actual ages, the first question might be:

'Okay, you found *Big Bills on the Sidewalk* to replace present Social Security, but how about Medicare and Medicaid? Isn't that the fastest growing threat?'

Compound Capitalism will solve the most threatening aspects of post age 67 Retirement Healthcare Security. **Yes, it is a big threat.**

"It's a puzzle, isn't it? We'll spend untold millions research to keep people living longer and longer, but almost nothing to ensure that they can live those years in reasonable comfort. Until we acknowledge those contradictions and change the policies that flow from them, more than a few children will impoverish themselves to help pay for the care of parents who have outlived their savings."

—Lillian B. Rubin, 60 On Up: *The Truth About Aging in America*, Beacon Press

With costs on the rise, our solution puts $4,000 in a Retirement Healthcare Account for every newborn citizen or every new naturalized citizen. You will remember that we are using 4,000,000 annually as the number of new participants. Therefore, $16 billion annually is required to make that investment.

Retirement Healthcare Accounts (RHA) are not a replacement for pre-age 67 Medicare and Medicaid, but address the more unsustainable period of medical and healthcare expenditures—the future past age 67.

The post-67 cost averages are thus:

Hospital	32.8%
Nursing Home & Nursing	12.3%
Professional	26.5%
Drugs	6.3%
Dental	9.9%
Eye/Hearing	2.1%

Females live 8 years longer on average.

Compound Capitalism has offered a solution to the critical two-thirds of the problem, at no cost to the United States. Before going further, we think that is quite incredible. Just how much is incredible?

What would you say to another $82.4 Trillion Dollars?

Once again, if you multiply 4 million annual births and naturalizations times 67 years, the result is 268 millions of new citizens in the next 67 years. Each Retirement Healthcare Security Account contains $307,500 at age 67.

That means that *Compound Capitalism* will have provided 268,000,000 x $307,500 to citizen accounts for post retirement healthcare security. Want to guess how much that is? It's $82,410,000,000,000! That is $82 trillion, $410 billion dollars.

If you'd rather think in billions, that's 828,410 billions.

Please recall that we can now add this $82.410 trillions saved from *Retirement Healthcare Accounts* to the minimum* $164.820 trillions also saved by government enterprise in *Retirement Security Accounts*. The total saved by a switch to *Compound Capitalism* is $242.73 trillion dollars!

***We said minimum because RSA account holders can leave the principal at interest long past retirement age and the government sponsor retains 4% of the funds for its use.

Today the Congress was talking about saving $4 trillion dollars over ten years, slim pickings by comparison.

(Some 20% of these 268,000,000 insured persons, of course, will die before reaching age 67, but all non-vested trust amounts accrued in decedents RSA and RHA accounts will revert to the sponsoring Congressional agency, hopefully, only to the Debt Reduction Trust.)

(Mortality Tables are listed in the Appendix.) You can study the year-to-year mortality losses.)

Suzanne Barlyn writes in *The Wall Street Journal: Live Very, Very Long and Prosper*

"As more people live into their 90s and beyond, financial planning becomes even more important — and trickier.

At age 45, I can still call my grandmother to hear stories about the great Depression. She turned 97 this year. More than half a dozen close relatives have lived into their 90s, and that's just going back to my great-grandmother.

A long life, of course, can be a blessing. But financial advisers typically use a more daunting term: longevity risk. It's the reason that many develop retirement plans that assume their clients will live to at least age 93, reflecting the growth of the country's oldest population."

We are living much longer, thanks to what we know about medicine, diet, biology and biotechnology. The *Slaying the Dragon of Debt* issue of long-term healthcare sustainability is a major triumph.

When we talk about health, we often make analogies to financial health. Many think being born poor is a birth defect just as unhealthy as a heritable physical weakness carried through life. People are born into different circumstances. It is possible to modify inherited genetic, cultural, and financial differences, not in the sense of creating *'designer babies,'* but in the sense of changing human psychology—the rules-of-the-game.

Think of health and longevity. When government is comparable to a corporation with the charter to live forever, then it does not seem strange for citizen members of that enterprise to also revitalize that charter to be more consistent with their reality. The citizen however, unlike the government, will not live forever. Given that a citizen can face the future either demoralized or hopeful, the state of the State has a vital influence on the state of the mind—individually and culturally.

All the experts seem to agree that the state of the State cannot persist well when the common descriptive word is *'unsustainable.'* Most of us are capable of looking over today's transom at an ugly scene, and we don't have to be giants or stand on our toes. We need a better view.

Much better that you begin to accumulate a *Retirement Healthcare Account* (RHA) with invested capital of $4,000, also from birth or naturalization. After age 67, two-thirds your average lifetime medical expenses will occur and you will have accumulated $307,500—not heritable, but credited to support your post 67 healthcare needs.

This eliminates a long-term health insurance risk portion for newborns and new citizens. It enables legislators to have many more options in solving the shorter term pre-67 health insurance risks of those already born and naturalized, whether the pre-67 reform choices made are for health care support insurance, vouchers, major medical options, or some combination of proposals under present consideration. Whatever the choices, the longer-term post-age 67 *'unsustainable'* certainty is removed, a plus for legislators dealing with today's reform needs.

In the meantime, unless mentally unfit, few can easily imagine themselves excused from real world realities that impact the actual futures they confront. When they take the headsets off, or turn off the cell phone, their nation is saddled with a $19+ trillion dollar debt and the future of their retirement and healthcare security systems— **unsustainable**.

Chapter 8. Lifetime Educational Security

Increase our full potential from birth! Therefore, an annual investment of $12 billion dollars in Lifetime Educational Support, (LES), is also funded as part of the *Slaying the Dragon of Debt* included in *Compound Capitalism.*

You've been introduced to the Paul Romer concept of a 'non-rival good' being a recipe—something once released being available for use by all. This annual $12 billion dollar educational purchase becomes available to every world citizen, our own and others. Each individual won't use it all, of course, but the product of the money invested is forever available. In other words, the educational benefit available to all grows by $12 billion annually. That's monumental.

We encourage the support of the greater growth of pre K and K-12 education in language, science, math, engineering and technology, in conjunction with various forms of vocational, on-the-job, pre-professional and financial knowledge education.

Niall Ferguson, in his excellent history of finance, *Ascent of Money,* deplores the lack of financial literacy, everything from mortgage loans, credit cards, interest rates and other aspects of personal finance.

We also encourage the growth of educational technology innovations in math, science, technology, engineering and various forms of adult education. In the present, when economic growth is vital for financial stability, any other mindset is too much like a broken watch. The future of science, technology and education will either wind our watch, or it will clean our clock.

We must change the structure of government funded security programs, including education, not only because they are our largest national budget items, but also because the right concepts for change have come. Now we must restructure our thinking accordingly.

In any society, modern or ancient, individuals join together to accomplish goals they are not able to handle so well on their own, whether it was the ancient hunt of mammoth or tiger, or the modern group hunt for cooperation with other humans. We are social beings even when competitive. Neither individuals nor the cultural community are able to progress without the other, and often they must compromise. We seek individual goals through others. We have inherited that gene.

If one asks which comes first, having or being, we think that having is most able to free the spirit to become.

Education is a *'becoming'* opportunity. Predicting another person's behavior isn't a reliable science, of course, but it's the perfect reason for new options in education. Hopefully, in the near future people will say, *"I've fallen up, and I can't get down!"*

The best colleges have students from all states, so the bottom line is that students from every state need to compete on a level playing field of national standards. That is a fact. Among new options is the call for common educational standards. For example, the National Governor's Association and the Council of Chief State School officers combined with teachers to develop a standard for math and English.

We have 50 states spending an average of $156,000 per student K-12, 13 years at $12,000 each. If the investment is received with a high level of diligence, the taxpayers are rewarded. If, the student has been careless or inattentive, or the teacher average or poor, the money is down the drain. As reported by *The Economist* in 2011, a University of Washington study reported that spending on schools, adjusted for inflation, increased 29% from 1990 to 2005 **without any noticeable gain in achievement.**

At 7.69% of $156,000, *Compound Capitalism* proposes to assure that inattentive scholarship will not result in decreasing dependent citizenship and proposes to do so without any taxpayer cost sacrifice. Money invested early has a long educational payoff.

On the political front, *Race to the Top*, the Obama Administration's program, has created a $4.3 billion incentive to states to improve K-12 results. However, it isn't just states that are falling behind in responsibility for America's decline in international comparisons. It is because the whole nation is being measured in those rankings, not just the states.

We have 50 states, some 15,000 school districts, thousands of different curricula choices. While *Race to the Top* is an attempt to standardize, still too much is left up to choice rather than need. To date, only a dozen states have won large awards, mostly in the Eastern U.S. The president's goals include expanding the number and quality of charter schools, updating the way school districts evaluate teacher effectiveness, improving student data-tracking systems to help educators know what students have learned and what must be re-taught, and turning around thousands of the lowest-performing schools. *Compound Capitalism* applauds those efforts. We will help.

We hear and read much about educational choice, of charter schools, school vouchers and of improving the skill levels of both teachers and students. **While we are doing this, we can and should bring the best schools and teachers to our students, even before we are better able to bring our students to good schools and teachers.** After all, there are mushrooming examples that it takes more today than just a school voucher, because in most cases there are many more students desiring to go to a better school than there are available seats in those schools.

Many of you have read about Harlem's Success Network, where the demand is so great that admittance must be by luck-of-the-draw lottery. When New York City opened more than 100 charter schools, 40,000 families chose them. Sadly, however, another 40,000 are on the wait list.

So how do you pack up an entire charter school or a great group of teachers and send them off to waiting students?

Here is one way, reported by AP news on May 15, 2011.

Government unveils site to teach Web skills

WASHINGTON—A new Commerce Department Web site aims to give schools, libraries and job training centers the tools to help teach **computer and Internet skills** to Americans who are new to the Net. The site, www.digitalliteracy.gov, offers everything from basic Web surfing tips and banking tutorials to resume' building services and resources on combating cyber-bullies.

It is part of the push to ensure that all Americans have access to high-speed Internet connections and the skills needed to use them to compete in today's digital economy.

What logically follows that welcome announcement is that America doesn't really have to wait for a sufficient number of new teachers of science, technology, engineering and math (STEM) to be available to make progress, because excellent teachers teaching those subjects are already available. Once curricula are made available by government as Internet learning tools, then for teaching purposes, independently developed games, videos, etc., will surely follow.

How could one great second grade math teacher enhance the learning capabilities of all 4,000,000 second-graders in America, either during or after school hours? We've called this concept, *The Academic Edge Academy*.

Once parents know that an *Academy* seat for their child is available, at least in their own home, and that their government is using public money to make it universally available, then no amount of opposition is likely to make a difference in overcoming parental demand. Why wait for both children and adults to become more skilled and confident, when good teachers are already available?

How could that work with the entire K-12 curricula?

Assume that in grades 1-12 there are five fifty-minute classes each day. Twelve grade levels times five classes equal sixty different classes per year and per day. The school year is 180 days. Without advanced math, we multiply 60 times 180 and get 10,800 classes per year.

If we found the 60 best teachers, or even 60 very excellent ones, we could create *Internet* classrooms for the *Academic Edge Academy*. We know it is natural for every parent to want an extra *'edge'* for their child, so whether the child gains that extra plus of a great teacher at home or in the school classroom or library, its value will not be diminished. Perhaps it won't have all the advantage of the child being with a great teacher in an actual classroom, but it's much better than a bad teacher in a classroom. All pre-produced classes would include a balanced age and grade level group of students interacting with the teacher as is the norm in a live classroom.

Once educational networks are established in our era of the *Internet* and computers, the cost of adding users has little or no extra production cost to what has been established. According to our estimates, producing such a series for *Internet* delivery, including royalties for exceptional teachers, would require an initial budget of $600 million. Each of the superior teachers would receive as much as $1 million for a year's teaching. That accounts for $60 million of the $600 million. $9 million times 60 classes, or $540 million would be allocated for production costs.

Just for comparative purposes, you may be interested to know that the U.S. costs for K-12 education now exceed $600 billion dollars annually, a full thousand times more. We italicize *'annually'* because Internet versions might have to be revised only every four years, thus giving each Academic Edge class a three-year + shelf life. That would reduce the average annual production cost to an average of $200 million annually.

Depending on government action, such classes, in English, could be made available for worldwide use, either free or for a modest royalty.

We would anticipate that text materials would also be made available, with texts written by teams of subject experts already available. Because this cost is yet unknown, we anticipate a budgeted extra of $400 million, also every third year.

If you add these two investments together, *Lifetime Educational Support* (LES) has now invested only $1 billion of the first year's $12 billion dollar budget.

LES will allocate funds for some of the remaining $11 educational billions in the R&D section, regarding university academic support, vocational education, on-the-job skills training, professional training, STEM educational activities and student scholarship support. *Lifetime Educational Support* will assist these programs according to need.

Some of the budgeted $11 billion first year investment by *Lifetime Educational Support* will first have to be selected and proposals for grants evaluated. Initially, the U.S. government should designate a responsible umbrella organization, perhaps under joint Department of Commerce and Department of Education oversight.

Given the Department of Commerce's present involvement, and U.S. Department of Education's *Race to the Top* program, we are confident that imaginative and entrepreneurial individuals and enterprises will happily compete to justify the consideration and acceptance of their proposals. An excellent example one might check out now is Khan Academy, teaching math, science and other topics. Others succeeding in better education will be invited participants.

Some organizations like (SME) the Society of Manufacturing Engineers, have already considered how they might enhance professional and on-the-job training.

There are many science and engineering oriented associations and corporations leading today's quest for excellence. For example, Intel, IBM, Dow Chemical are just a few corporate examples. Cooperating associations like the *Invest in America Alliance* will do much to advance economic growth, innovation and competitiveness.

The Obama Administration showed *'grit'* in the Commerce Department response to enhance an education system clearly falling behind in the competitive marketplace, perhaps while anticipating potential objections from long entrenched interests to pour sand in the gears. It is, however, the logical response to playing the unwanted role of catch-up in a very competitive world economy. We need innovation and new ideas today.

We must move forward. The fact is that there are many changes now influencing the way in which people are taught that didn't exist a short time ago. Since the video age, for example, what began as sport instructional video training, golf, football, etc., has now advanced rapidly, including teaching U.S. military personnel through 3-D videos featuring virtual reality warriors as action teachers for soldiers, all via highly sophisticated interactive video games. The soldier can now learn and practice without getting shot or killed. We would have to say, that is a definite plus.

We also know already that interactive video is becoming a convenient and useful means of having subject experts teach laboratory techniques in science classrooms—without explosions of course, another plus.

Is virtual reality in general or professional education far behind, or has it already arrived? Studies report that participants in virtual reality experiments quickly embrace the life-like reality of becoming integrated into their own learning experiences. Time will tell.

Not that such make-believe standing alone can earn a livelihood, pay the rent or the mortgage, make the participant become well educated, responsible or one iota better looking, but it does nonetheless suggest that we will find ourselves fully immersed in startling new learning experiences we could have barely imagined just yesterday. Perhaps the virtual world of the very near future will become the new model peer group of human fulfillment? Who knows?

In the meantime, **LES is a voucher program for every person wanting to learn in America,** including adults who would like a second chance, not only in repeating every learning opportunity that passed them by, but also new educational units oriented toward vocational, on-the-job or professional training. In the privacy of one's own home there is nothing to prevent an adult from repeating his/her own K-12 past in the much enhanced modern format. In a very real sense, every home becomes its own charter school with its own voucher program. It is a guaranteed avenue toward advancing one's own knowledge. Perhaps it is among the better responses to the present debates over *"all lives matter."* Lives that matter start at home.

For those of you who have become curious about the potential future of the virtual world, *Infinite Reality* by Drs. Jim Blaskovich and Jeremy Bailenson is both challenging and revealing. Bailenson heads up the Virtual Human Interaction Lab at Stanford University. What has already been done is more than you might know. Unless you study the virtual world on a regular basis, you will be surprised at how it will change young lives.

We think virtual classrooms and *Internet* delivery of educational curricula are key technologies for the future. The LES function of *Compound Capitalism* proposes a budget of $5 billion dollars annually to research, develop and test these technologies. This subtraction reduces the LES budget to $6 billion dollars. Later in this book, you will see how the balance is invested.

In the interim, we do not live in a virtual world, at least not yet. Unless mentally unfit, few of us can easily imagine ourselves excused from real world realities and responsibilities that impact the actual futures we confront.

When each of us remove our virtual head-sets, our nation is still saddled with a $19+ trillion debt. The futures of the present retirement and healthcare security systems are *'unsustainable.'* This is reality, not virtual reality! **We need more than a new TV head-set, we need a reset—of reinvigorating capitalist revival.**

Chapter 9. Compound Capitalism—Human Capital: Inheritance, Psychological Security, Family Nurturing & Peer Group Socialization

Human capital resources are born as children, so let's look first at the human capital of *Compound Capitalism. Capital, like any tool, depends much on its use. First, it has to be recognized as an asset.*

Perhaps the first to be internationally recognized for his focus on human capital was the late economist Dr. Gary Becker of the University of Chicago, whose insights made him a Nobel Laureate.

In a 1989 lecture, Becker described it this way:

"To most of you, capital means a bank account, one hundred shares of IBM, assembly lines or steel plants. These are all forms of capital in the sense that they yield income and other useful outputs over a long period of time … but I am going to talk about a different sort of capital. Schooling, a computer training course, expenditures on medical care and lectures on the virtues of punctuality and honesty are capital, too, in the sense that they improve health, raise earnings or add to a person's appreciation of literature over much of his or her lifetime. Consequently, it is fully in keeping with the capital concept as traditionally defined to say that expenditures on education, training, medical care, etc. are investments in capital … however, these produce human, not physical or financial capital, because you cannot separate a person from his or her knowledge, skills, health or values the way it is possible to move financial and physical assets while the owner stays put."

So, it is in this sense, too, that the proposed solution of human-productivity tax credits is much oriented toward

Becker's Nobel winning concept of 'human capital.' Becker is also rightfully famous for his further development of the hidden resources concept and the book: Human Capital.

The underlying claim of this writing is that 'sovereign wealth' is too narrowly viewed. Some sovereignty rests solely on the degree of force or control the rulers have over citizens and resources. Some nations so-called 'sovereign wealth funds' benefit from control of wages, accidents of geography and/or from resources of nature, oil, gold, diamonds or other mineral wealth in the ground, or even benefit from a more fertile ground itself or through reliable and adequate rainfall. Other nations less naturally endowed also can benefit, but more from cultural and human resources which form a primary basis of their 'sovereign wealth.' Japan is a good example.

Compound Capitalism therefore asserts that the citizens of all nations can be 'shareholders' in whatever the human, geographical, natural or cultural assets of their nations are, whether or not they have a legally recognized real property shareholder stake in their particular portfolio of assets. We hope they, too, will adopt *Compound Capitalism*.

That is because a person cannot easily be separated from his or her point of view toward the world. What we add to Gary Becker's insight is that expectations of the future are part of a person's knowledge and unquestionably a part of the mental health aspects of developing skills throughout a lifetime. We would be remiss not to credit Becker with a significant part of this argument, but faith in the productive human asset future is a wholly different faith than our hope that the government will step in to avert an old age debt disaster will have both a plan and the means to do so. Becker might also be the first to conclude that enhancing productivity emotionally and in spirit helps to insure its actual political realization of humans having a more formal economic value.

Interestingly enough, by different routes, both the UN and the World Bank have come to Becker's conclusion based on significant further studies, that the real wealth of nations, regardless of other influences, is their human dimension, especially their young citizenry. Every nation's most valuable assets are its children.

That is the essence of The World Bank's 2006 book, *Where is the Wealth of Nations?* It's a much different emphasis and conclusion from the traditional land, labor and produced capital explanation and describes a different kind of natural resource. World Bank puts it this way:

"The estimates of total wealth — including produced, natural and human and institutional capital — suggest that the human capital and the value of institutions (as measured by rule of law) constitute the largest share of wealth in virtually all countries."

In the World Bank Study, they weighed the wealth of the world as 77% human capital, 5% in natural resources and 18% in produced capital. Much unlike assets buried in the ground, human asset value has the potential to grow, whereas the former only diminish with time. Human capital has the opportunity to grow, not only in quantity, but also in quality, and to benefit an entire society, both cooperatively and by individual measure.

It is only the productivity of human enterprise that is the source of economic growth. It is whether or not these human assets are well educated and productively invested that establishes present and future outlooks, and with it, the prospects of their nation—any nation.

One might easily say that human differences are required in order to make striving possible, accomplishment recognizable. The unique human model which each of us represents also shares much that is common. We share our shortcomings and our virtue. Without this inherent margin of difference, the quality of our choices would not be important. In the final measure, there are choices of difference that refer to the morality of those choices. In those measures we can go beyond or fall short of the arithmetic—our sum of original gifts. It is in the flowering of gifts that we fulfill our purpose. To encourage this, we must take care not to overlook gifts that are already there, the unseen 'acres of diamonds.'

Therefore, as we now consider the sources for different kinds of sovereign shareholder diamonds: genes, families, cultures, peer groups, social networks; all of whose positive benefits not only grow, but whose growth compounds by reason of ever increasing numbers of shareholders. Think of a financial Facebook. In this new equation, we consider various outcomes and forms of compounding; compounding wealth, health, knowledge and culture.

On having his own DNA sequenced, noted psychologist Steven Pinker commented on the results in *My Genome, Myself,* published Jan 11, 2009 in *The New York Times*:

"We are shaped by our genes in ways that none of us can directly know ... each of us is dealt a unique hand of tastes and aptitudes, like curiosity, ambition, empathy, a thirst for novelty or security, a comfort level with the social or the mechanical or the abstract. Some opportunities we come across click with our constitutions and set us along a path in life."

What Dr. Pinker described is something remarkably surprising and different today. At the firm, 23andMe, one can now get a basic genome screening for $99. Why do people want to know?

It was Dorothy Parker who said, *"There is no cure to curiosity."* What would you do if someone looked inside your child's genome to discover three terrific 'memes' nobody would ever imagine finding or having: retirement income security, retirement healthcare security and lifetime educational support, all already built into his/her genome? Who wouldn't pay $99 to discover that?

At birth, we don't know how smart we are, how healthy we will be, what nutrition our bodies will receive, how we will be encouraged, educated, motivated, how timely, few or many our opportunities will be, or how we will be regarded by others or how others are judged by us.

That's quite a lot not to know in advance, but even then, certain circumstances provide clues. Much of what will happen in each future requires neither a crystal ball nor a fortune-teller, because we know the outlook each person has is shaped by the outlook of those closest to them. Some of life's chances are genetic, of course, some influenced by the educational attainment of the family and some conditioned by a nurturing environment— and often much more by peer groups.

This is not to say, of course, that exceptional individuals don't also overcome exceptional obstacles, but, then again, they are not the norm.

But what if we could change the norm for tomorrow?

Family, Peers, Psychology & Culture

All mankind is not created equal, not even by the mighty Gods of all religions, and certainly not so by parents. Two children in the same family are never equal. Even identical twins have clear differences. Modern science has established, almost beyond any doubt, that genetics may have a lesser role to play in our make-up than was previously imagined, even though half our genes are inherited from parents.

What if we could change the circumstances for all the individuals who have anything at all to do with the outlook equations—parents, culture and peers? What if we could use untapped resources to provide the necessary spark?

Forgetting anger or rebellion against inequalities within the natural inherited order, we can, nonetheless, create certain equalities when we build human social constructs. A citizen socialization incentive program like *Compound Capitalism* is such a man-made instrument—and an inheritance.

Parents, and other family members make choices for children all the time, not that those that influence children always know best, but because it's expected. Even outside influences make decisions for children. Nobody asks parents, nor should they, if it is proper to endow children with a natural propensity for inherited characteristics, even the bad ones. So why shouldn't parents also have the freedom to create their children as inheritors of wealth—both financial, moral and emotional?

Family and Parental Capital—A Money Mutation

Families Nurturing Well

Most children start off in families. We don't select our
parents, but they selected us. Families, no matter how they
are constituted, greatly or generously endowed, still count.
Children need solid, dependable relationships, particularly
kinship relationships. When we can smile at babies, they
do better, emotionally and physically. The emotional
environments in which children mature , especially in the
pre-peer group period, is crucial. To be held in esteem and
to esteem others provides an immediate atmosphere for
growth, not regression. If one begins life with the simple
dignity of human ambitions, parents must then continually
ask if their roles in optimizing that dignity is being
realized? It's a time of opportunity with lasting effect on
our children. In particular, family structures need strong
models. Modern life is so much more than just surviving.
People are surviving longer, of course, but are they living
better? We believe they can and that *Compound Capitalism*
is powerful enough that they will.

A question hangs over families, asking if they are to be
caregivers or caretakers? Demands of increasing
expectation have fallen more directly on modern families,
both single parents and couples often working two jobs.

Despite many well-publicized negative problems,
particularly in inner-city environments, families remain a
significant hope for the future. If we could make *'social
security'* a self-fulfilling general term that would cover the
entire range of ages in our society, we would have
answered a critical social capital question, making us a
more skillful society of family caregivers. Both biology and
family culture are transmitted from parents to children,

one encoded in the DNA and another in the family culture —its pattern of behavior and its reflections of the general culture.

Social capital is often missing in the equation, because both families and societies must be based on trust. Trust is earned. If trust is to exist between individuals, generations or cultures, moral norms must also be shared. Moral norms are our human tuning forks for individuals and cultures. They are the true music of life.

In that sense, man is like a self-tuning piano that must constantly refine the ability to stay in harmony with its natural gifts. Such are the unrealized potentials for the productivity diamonds that are born with each child through *Compound Capitalism.* One might say it is the sum of unrealized gifts not yet given the power of choices. Man is intended, if nothing else, to do good works—to create harmony.

Compound Capitalism is intended to also solve key sources of overhanging debt problems, and by so doing, to further awaken people toward better and more successful individual futures for themselves, asking each of us to think more about what we can contribute, not what we have coming.

A decision made for children that will multiply the choices they can make on their own is one of the more positive attributes any parent can pass to a child. It is a case of the **'invisible hand'** truly at work, and in this case, a loving hand. A man-made mutation that stacks the deck in your child's favor is any geneticist's dream. Could we call this natural selection, or even parental selection? A hit movie of the future may be *"Honey, I've built up the kids."*

It is only because we care about the future that we are moral beings. Why do we socialize our children, exhort them to better things, teach them, urge restraint and tell them right from wrong? Those lessons are true, no matter the culture. When, for whatever reason, we think the future does not merit learning or teaching systems of value, life will be a sorry mess. Values are shared among the human species no matter what a person's religion, or none. We base the meaning of life on the belief that accomplishing something good, rather than bad, is our noble purpose. No matter what one's stated religion, or none, the Golden Rule of treating others as we would want to be treated is a proven and reliable starting point.

Even without debate, all parents favor passing on a legacy of stable inheritance rather than financial obligation. No poll taken among parents would likely prove otherwise. *"I don't want to be a burden on my children,"* is the universal wish of the aging.

We believe building and maintaining family strengths will be mightily enhanced by each family member when all know in advance there is something much better in store for each of them. Families will have new reasons to build solidarity and staying power. For one example, along the lines of family stability, we believe marriages will be stronger, out-of-wedlock births will be minimized, both because apathy and self-disregard will be modified toward a better end result outcomes.

Leisure time and avocations should take on new and broader meanings and people will realize a newfound ability to develop skills through more diverse activity or new vocations or entrepreneurship. Financial resources will better combine with opportunity?

Youngsters born into dysfunctional or poverty plagued families or single-parent households have already experienced a cycle of dependency. Their education has surely suffered. *Compound Capitalism* also draws upon Becker's *'human capital'* in a new way. Parents will recognize that there is a better future for their children almost immediately. As such, it is available intellectually for even the most educationally or culturally disadvantaged parent to grasp instinctively. It immediately shouts out:

"Thank God, my kid will have a chance!"

Meeting a challenge of changing the odds requires that no available resource, nor any child, be left behind. There is no means testing in the womb. Means testing introduces legislative discrimination into democratic politics, putting the engines of discriminatory politics and representative government on a collision course, an unwanted and disastrous crash so easily prevented by switching tracks now. This is a particularly important change for psychological outlooks, most certainly for those we define as the *'working poor,'* a group which will be altered for life by *Compound Capitalism.*

Despite references to disadvantaged families, you will note that there is no attempt to redistribute wealth, income, or to mimic any welfare related entitlement program. This is opportunity, not welfare, and exists exclusively by making incentive a more positive reconcilement to the known dismal future of Social Security and Medicare as structured today.

Telling a teen-age, unmarried mother to go out and get a job might be very bad advice. But she might be much more willing to get the training needed for a job that best fits her situation; both reassured and inspired because the future of her family is no longer bleak. Breaking the cycle of dependency is better begun in the mind and with an unmistakable symbol of hope. We can think of none stronger than *Compound Capitalism*.

The Power of Peers

Perhaps the nurture role of the family is less important than experts once imagined, because for better or worse, children so quickly join other groups more like themselves in age. If the predominant peer group majority are offspring of disillusioned or despairing parents, it's not likely to be a positive influence carried into the peer group group socialization process. **Conversely, if the entire peer group has been made better off at birth, we believe both parents and peer groups will experience immediate benefits.**

When did people begin saying "you know," "I couldn't care less," or start wearing extra long and baggy shorts— or Twitter and Facebook? One very good answer is that we are all influenced, perhaps more than we know, by both our peer groups and social media.

The nature vs. nurture argument is still with us, of course, but leading psychologists and educators are in basic agreement and recognition of the key importance of peer groups in the socializing of children.

The belief today is that peer groups become dominant influences in the socialization and maturation of children and that positive productivity, or its emotional negatives, exist in peer groups in both real and potential forms. This reflects the diligent research of more than a single author's imagination, particularly experts writing about the psychology and socialization of children. **(Steven Pinker, Judith Rich Harris, Tina Rosenberg, James Surowicki, Jeremy Bailenson, Malcolm Gladwell, Martin Nowak, Margaret Brewer and others**), just to name a few good examples. We attest that their insights are on the mark, not necessarily subject to mathematical proof, at least not yet, but we think them provable psychologically, in the lives of each of us.

We, too, in an attempt to change peer group direction, are interested in re-engineering our heirs, (and yours) but mostly to realize the best of heritable potentials already inherent within them. We are not talking about creating designer babies. We add no other data element to the mix, no magic gene other than the conviction of the insight that better peer groups can also be created at birth. **We are not attempting to order up blue or brown-eyed children, only more eyes filled with greater wonder and fewer tears.**

Whether we should have added new forms of social networking, such as Facebook, MySpace, or Twitter directly to the current peer group definition, we don't yet know for certain, but one must agree there are strong forces at work beyond genetics, parents, peer groups and cultures. Instant and intimate networking groups are now being added to our culture—for good and bad. To one degree or another, these will influence us in increasingly subtle and not so subtle ways.

Parental example helps to establish the home part of the nurturing equation. Therefore, with (LES) Lifetime Educational Support added to the ingredients, it might soon follow that parents with an asset of strong education beamed into every home that wants it—are more likely to instill that influence in their children. We hope to provide 'distance learning' opportunities for home viewing developed by experts, helping all to be better parents. It is training for both parent and child. It will certainly be easier for parents who have not regarded education highly, or whose ability to do so up till now has been limited. We think that parental support assets will take their place in family nurturing.

We can solve the problem of increasing the potential of all age groups by allowing the opportunity for personal accomplishment to flourish. Unbelievably, it is that simple. We want to internalize an incentive for success that is built into every human model and put it to work—tomorrow.

Science will extend, purposefully, perhaps by many years, lives of our own choosing. Given little choice in the matter of extended years, would we rather choose prosperity for our future, or barely making ends meet? Even if our genes never engineer children who will live much longer, we will all live longer just the same, because someone is already engineering cures and treatments for the major childhood and adult diseases that are today's killers.

Compound Capitalism is not only powerful enough to make that accomplishment self-fulfilling, but it is a latent property right within each of us. Using it may not make each life a masterpiece, but as individual works of art, life's brushstrokes will be much improved.

Compound Capitalism is an acknowledgement of shareholder citizenship long overdue, only different in structural design and productive purpose. However, its support argument does not require agreement that obligations occurring far into the future are best handled by using current income for fulfillment. Quite the contrary is a preferred response. The public does have money for social purposes, but not unlimited money for everyone's special current need or envy fulfillment. That's why the time has come for *Compound Capitalism.*

Our position accepts that there are trade-offs in life when one good is chosen in lieu of another—or when fate deals differing hands to each of us. There is no full-service cornucopia of *'make a wish'* granting. Every *'compound capital'* penny counts toward increasing productivity, not welfare. This line of thinking does not favor any special interest group, political party, any particular category of individual or any type of corporation or business, but is valuable to all, as every individual gets *'just'* treatment; hardly possible under any other definition of democracy, constitutional or otherwise. This is truly an example of equality into which every future American citizen can be born, if we demand it. Furthermore, the self-interest of politics cannot help but admire a system that produces both personal and national wealth in the bargain, with equal treatment under the law—and all with *Big Bills Found on the Sidewalk.*

There are many good social purposes, only some of which merit such universal support. We firmly believe a great nation can and should sustain a system that provides bedrock retirement income, retirement healthcare and educational benefits upon which further societal attainment can be built.

The Psychological Self

Explaining Compound Capitalism to Children

In comparison to the past, *Compound Capitalism* seems a fantasy—too good to be true. Perhaps some readers are old enough to remember the 1955-60 popular TV show, *The Millionaire*. For viewers back then, the fabulously wealthy John Beresford Tipton, whom we never saw, but whose voice was that of Paul Frees, would summon his secretary Michael Anthony, played by Marvin Miller. With the spacious Tipton estate of Silverstone in the background, Tipton explained to Anthony who would be that week's beneficiary. Viewers invariably dreamt of what an incredible thing it would be if Michael Anthony rang their doorbell and delivered a million dollars from John Beresford Tipton.

Times have changed, and a million dollars isn't worth quite as much as it was then, but by the same token, Mr. Anthony delivered only 205 checks in six years. From it's own first six years, *Compound Capitalism* proposes to deliver 24,000,000 future checks, each valued at $922,500!

In the future, the specific version of Michael Anthony's TV visit that becomes the way in which children will be introduced to Compound Capitalism will undoubtedly take many forms. DVDs, games, books, are obvious means of teaching. It will obviously be discussed in classrooms and certainly in casual settings among family and peers. Exactly when is the best time for learning will vary, because each child is different. **We are confident that good news travels fast. We have stacked the deck.**

Does United States leadership believe that young people will respond positively to an investment made in their future well-being, an investment made before the young citizen's productivity has had any opportunity to make its hoped for payoff back to their nation?

Political leadership already believes that happier citizens are more productive citizens. Productivity isn't just an ability to turn out ideas, innovations, products or services, although that is part of it. The part that is harder to measure is how much more productive are citizens who can be taught from birth that:

- Their fellow citizens have faith in them to be good citizens.
- Their government believes that happier citizens are more productive.
- Their government believes that more productive citizens pay more taxes.
- Their government believes that more productive citizens require fewer government services.
- Their government believes that secure citizens contribute more to their own families, to their communities, to the nation and to the world.
- Their government believes that happier citizens are healthier, as they have more to look forward to.
- Their government believes that a populace more widely invested in their own system of democratic market capitalism is more likely to feel part of an investor class, a status making one more likely to embrace the challenges of a interconnected world.
- Their government believes that those involved in wealth creation benefit from growth beyond U.S. borders.
- Their government believes that an 'investor class' is a much more effective future distinction than one so negatively described by more common terms like 'mill hunk' or low wage earner.

• Their government and their civil society believe productive people are less prone to negative activities, including criminal behavior.

Well trained experts in cognitive and child psychology will have much to say and learn themselves, regarding when particular elements are best introduced, and how.

Steven Pinker says that no foreseeable robot can match an ordinary person's ability to recognize unexpected objects and situations, decide what to do about them in unanticipated ways, all the while exchanging information with other humans.

Dr. Pinker goes on to say: *"Babies are born into the world not knowing a word of the language being spoken around them. Yet in three years, without the benefit of lessons, most of them will be talking a blue streak, with a vocabulary of thousands of words, a command of the grammar of the spoken vernacular and a proficiency with the sound pattern."*

If the acquisition of new language is a triumph for children and learning a few words and phrases like *skin-in-the-game, capitalist, capitalize, shareholder, stakeholder, interest, compound interest and profit* is bound to change a future adult's view of life's pursuit of happiness. When the adolescent mind recognizes later on in life what an incredibly lucky start they had, even before they could possibly grasp what it might mean. they will cheer, and with tears on their cheeks.

Considering Dr. Pinker's insights about how quickly children learn language, and perhaps right from the start, we should be repeating: ***"You are a stockholder, you are a shareholder, you are a stockholder, you are a shareholder. You have skin-in-the-game."***

Inheriting capitalism's compound benefits may be as much psychological as financial. There are no cookie-cutter children, equal in genetic advantages, brainpower, parental capability, cultural environment, etc., and no state can change those differences easily. What a state can do is to provide everyone with opportunities, incentives, reward and respect. Even so, it cannot control the reactions of different humans to the same opportunity—but it can and should, change the odds for better results in the aggregate.

Moreover, we have continued to evolve with an even more important visionary premise that is well grounded in human experience and proven time and again. That 'truth' is this:

People who have an enhanced self-image and solid prospects for their individual futures will tend to recreate themselves as self-fulfilling prophecies of greater productivity. At least they have a reason to try.

To understand the powerful motivation of enhanced self-esteem, you don't have to ask the greatest coaches, the greatest athletes, the greatest high-tech innovators, the greatest artists or even the best psychologists to give memorable and moving testimony of the powers of motivation. Ask anyone, from the grocer to the symphony conductor, from the factory worker to the union president —because they all know the value of an inspired outlook. What you will hear is story after story confirming the fact that a vision of bright light at the end of the tunnel changes the entire trip—the fact is that one's self-image or attitude changes everything.

The champion professional golfer and now network commentator Johnny Miller recalled on Golf Talk Live, and with considerable nostalgia and emotion, that as a child, his father always called him *'Champ.'* He recalls that as he matured as both a golfer and a young man, that the persistence of that salutation *'Champ'* from his dad, helped to build his self-esteem. Miller states how that lesson carried over when he taught his own children, how important it is that parents make an effort to build confidence.

Cultural Inheritance

In 2007, Dr. Freeman Dyson wrote his famous paper, *Our Biotech Future*. Here, he is talking about cultures.

"Now, after three billion years, the Darwinian interlude is over. It was an interlude between two periods of horizontal gene transfer. The epoch of Darwinian evolution based on competition between species ended about ten thousand years ago, when a single species, Homo sapiens, began to dominate and reorganize the biosphere. Since that time, cultural evolution has replaced biological evolution as the main driving force of change."

People within a nation often have certain identifying features, characteristics that set them aside from citizens in another nation, perhaps even a bordering neighbor. We are not speaking of physical, religious or ethnic differences, but varied and shared human features, including differing moral values or outlooks. We hope to focus this insight on changes for the better, even if it requires changing points-of-view with some aspects of the past, including belief systems. We need to remember that we are a democratic capitalist nation—a republic yet unfulfilled by reason of too few shareholders. We too, must evolve, into a stronger organism.

The United States of America, since the beginning, even before political separation from the British, featured immigrants that were first and foremost of independent and entrepreneurial spirit; religiously, politically and economically—as well as by geographic origin. Even those who first came as indentured labor came with the hope that they could earn a better societal status from their efforts. We made our share of mistakes along that road.

More significant than single individuals improving their prospects through effort and change in viewpoint is the amazing cumulative result of many individuals striving simultaneously for better futures and succeeding through their cooperative effort. One easily begins to realize that *'compound interest'* isn't only a description of how money put to work grows larger over time, but perhaps more importantly, how **the efforts of human capital compound and grow when employed productively, also over time and by ever growing numbers of citizens.**

The same compounding is true when nurturing a new political dialog. As a nation we can't easily convince young people, by just a few words, that we have faith in their potential for being great future citizens with resources for future contributions, even with very carefully chosen words. Better for a nation's leaders to show and tell them simultaneously, without forgetting that future citizen's contributions will include tax revenues as well as varied other contributions, all rewarding thoughtful leadership at the same time.

Citizens already have an earned shareholder heritage, and keep in mind also, that we have stated that many of the words in this book are intended to have more than one meaning. You've been given more than one definition for recipes vs. ideas, interest vs. interests, capitalists and capital, economic integration and globalization. At this point you recognize some of the intended differences in meaning.

In the future, *Compound Capitalism* imagines we will soon look at the persons we meet on the street, in the supermarket or in the classroom in an entirely new light. When one's already well earned capitalist ownership interests are more easily recognized, perhaps with each person wearing a more visible facial badge of pride, it *will* gain status, power of place, and become an inherited characteristic, a new peer 'meme' that we will both inherit and share with others.

A newborn child probably doesn't have any obvious economic aspirations, like capitalist interests, but she does recognize nuances. In infancy, profit/loss comparisons are measured in being well fed, loved and made physically and mentally secure. A more nourishing home and cultural environment goes a long way.

In our imagined future, we will compound interests as well as interest; we will compound ideas, innovation, incentives, retirement and health security resources, education, governance, cooperation, R&D efforts, intellectual property, immigration opportunity and entrepreneurship.

Adult Psychology: How About Us?

The parents or parent—even the concerned adult who explains *Compound Capitalism* to a child realizes a couple of difficult, hard to deal with facts. Present parents still have the U.S. government's old promises, Social Security, Medicare and Medicaid.

But those facts are history. Parents whose incomes are limited because of prior decisions , or just bad luck, are instantly made richer by the knowledge that their children's futures will be much different from their own. While perhaps an occasion for wishing otherwise, a moment's regret that they had not missed this opportunity for themselves, *Compound Capitalism* is also a continuing and positive reminder to parents that people and governments keep on learning, both how to live better and how to live more productive lives. That is what we mean when we talk about the advance of civilization.

Perhaps more difficult to explain within the context of a family is how a particular moment in time, a date of birth, can separate children in the same family, perhaps kids only a year or two apart, as *Compound Capitalism* applies to citizens not yet born or not yet naturalized. Is this fair? **It is better than fair, because you will now be more likely to actually get what you thought you would receive at retirement, not less.**

For any who might wince at the comparative prospect of getting exactly what they expected, you are not short-changed. In addition you will receive extra benefits immediately. One of course, is this one, *Lifetime Educational Support.*

The intangible/tangible benefits, also large, are the values you place on having created a better future for all Americans. There are extra benefits that may take less than a generation to realize. Let's repeat that all psychological and emotional benefits start immediately, not 67 years from now.

A *Compound Capitalism* Recap: Looking Ahead

Between ages 18 and 28, most of us already born will probably begin our adult work. The same is true for those born tomorrow. Others among us have been working for forty or less years, some slightly more.

Someone who is born tomorrow has 18 to 28 years to begin a more formal life of work. **(The average age is 23.)** Whenever the actual dates, those persons will begin or have already begun to pay payroll taxes for older citizens' Social Security, Medicare and Medicaid. That may describe the current you.

Those who are already 67 or older will probably have traveled to the happy hunting ground before these younger persons start working 23 years hence, because 67 + 23 is 90. Those already working would have already paid for the benefits of those now retired, and they will continue to do so until their own retirements.

Young people don't want to diminish their chances in life just so generations who came before them can get theirs. Too many young people think their chances of achieving the good life are not nearly as good as were their parent's chances. And when their parents have gained no obvious share of the good life, their children think there is absolutely no chance at all.

Over time, this pressure becomes stressful and depressing. Stress has a high health cost. Also, people can easily lose their objectivity when they worry about their future, too often giving insufficient thought to the present. We are approaching this stress point. Right now, too many of our citizens are not feeling positive about the future.

But the question itself does call for a more detailed examination of just how long it might take for the greatest number of people to gain the most advantages. Let's start by thinking about ages different from where their own personal age is now.

The average U.S. income per person today is $50,000+. If that increases normally until tomorrow's newborn child is the average age of 23, for example, the average income in 2039 will be around $60,000-$70,000. Even if the payroll tax did not increase from 12.8% or apply to a larger gross income, it would then be nearing $8,000-$10,000.

Tomorrow's newborns in 2039 will begin paying annually the same sum, or more than is to be invested for them at their birth to pay for their own *retirement income security*. This seems fair. Nobody gets a free pass, at least not yet.

Nonetheless, when you subtract all the persons 67 or older today (90+ then) from those who will be 23 in 23 short years, then all those persons now 44 will themselves be 67 in 2039.

Sticking to this formula, for those at age 44 in 2039, they have been working for perhaps only 21 years themselves.

This *'age-jockeying'* exercise makes clear that tomorrow's newborn child will be supporting the retirement security of older others in just 23 short years, even though *Compound Capitalism's* retirement security was established at birth. *So, the second point is that tomorrow's newborn will* have vastly narrowed the present working adult's period of transition by stabilizing longer-term security.

What is also different and better is that by eliminating the longer-term unsustainable quality of unfunded Social

Security, Medicare and Medicaid, those presently under 44 and working may then look forward to having payroll taxes either significantly reduced or fully eliminated during their working lifetimes, and then everyone following them may pay nothing in payroll taxes. That carries the prospect that all incomes could be increased by as much as 12.8% in 44 years or less.

Employers presently recover their portion of payroll tax by control of wages employees are paid or by raising the prices of goods and services. When payroll deductions are nonexistent, incomes and products can better reflect their actual worth.

We make the case that *Compound Capitalism* is better than fair, because you've never had any government guarantee that your Social Security expectation would be honored, and in fact yours has probably already been changed, perhaps more than once. It never was truly funded.

So, because of what *Compound Capitalism* has proposed, you are now likely to receive exactly what you expected, guarantee or not. That's because this freeing-up of long-term debt liability has taken the pressure off, enough so that you can regain confidence in getting what you thought you would.

You will like that because you will be getting much more than you had reason to hope for, not less. The fact that newer citizens will fare better is a condition of the passage of time, with history as witness. Every generation has advantages over previous ones through advances in longevity, health, education, etc. No study made to date fails to note the widespread increases in standards-of-living over time. The diets of today's poor, for example, are better than those of prior kings.

An undemocratic response to *Compound Capitalism* would be for present citizens to insist upon the utopian delusion that every person must benefit from another person's hard work or good fortune, no matter how or when they got it. **That would be an embrace of socialism and the loss of *The American Dream. We are capitalists!***

Happily, there are means of participation for those born before *Compound Capitalism.* You now have *Lifetime Educational Support* that you can use no matter what your present age. Further, a growing economy will enhance your use of that continuing education and improve your job and income prospects along with your pursuits of happiness.

There has already been a discussion of the influence of peer groups in the socialization of children. Remind yourself that childhood peer groups are usually similar in age to the other children in that group, so whatever has influenced every member as an individual prior to their having joined their own peer group will also tend to carry that impact over into whatever other peer groups that individual joins throughout her life. In a short time, the heritable plans discussed in this book will have become a continuous socializing factor for every child, no matter what their newest peer group may become. Anyway, by the time your child joins a peer group, people will have figured out all kinds of innovative ways to talk about the future.

Most of all we will compound the hopes and opportunity of our greatest resource, children.

Chapter 10. Looking for Big Bills Left on the Sidewalk

We have now already invested $60 billion dollars annually. (We intend to invest $40 billion more annually which will be explained further on. You must be more than a little curious? How did we find all this money, these *Big Bills Left on the Sidewalk*?

$500 billions plus to start! *But where did all this money come from? Amazing! Are you wondering?*

In case you didn't read the preface, the late Mancur Olson, Jr. wrote a famous paper, *Big Bills Left on the Sidewalk,* portraying two economists coming upon a $100 bill lying on the sidewalk. When the junior one bent to pick it up, the senior and wiser economist retorted:

"If that were real, someone else would already have picked it up!"

Perhaps the older professor was a Marxist—at least a socialist, but we will encourage real capitalists, not only to be on the alert for such easy money, but also to quickly pick it up.

In their book, *Infinite Reality,* Jim Blaskovich and Jeremy Bailenson discuss the studies of Dan Smart's experiments and what he called *'motivational blindness.'* Smart's book, *The Invisible Gorilla,* takes its name from these studies. This experiment has been repeated many times, both at the University of Illinois and Stanford University.

Imagine yourself as a participant. We ask you to watch a video of two teams passing a basketball among team members and to count the times each team's players passed the ball. Sounds easy.

Do you think you would notice if a gorilla walked on the court among the players? (A life-sized person in a gorilla costume.) You are not warned about the gorilla.

In the video, the gorilla walks into the middle of the players, beats its chest, and walks off the scene. Then the video is shown to its participants, you included. Forty-six percent of the other viewers do not report seeing the gorilla. This blindness, not seeing things that are obviously there, repeats itself in life.

But when shown the video for a second time, literally half the viewers shriek in wild surprise after being asked to look for the gorilla. **We are asking our leadership to see the gorilla—the *Big Bills* that are there, *Left on the Sidewalk*.**

Sometimes when we look for *Big Bills Left on the Sidewalk*, we don't look hard enough, or we get lazy. Other times we might think something looks like a *Big Bill*, but isn't. Most of the time, *Big Bills* are what they look like, but we just don't take that in. We must learn to seize opportunity.

The Big Bills 'saved money concept' is the ongoing resource theme of this book. We will discuss other sources of *Big Bills Left on the Sidewalk* in the chapter titled *Other Big Bills Left on the Sidewalk,* and then discuss how new sources of income might be brought to light and recovered. We needn't think the *Big Bills* we will consider next are the last or only available funds, but they are the *Big Bills* most readily available in such a large amount.

The debt crisis is now predictable. We can see it as clearly as the gorilla in the room. It is also beating its chest to gain our attention. If we add lack of confidence to the mix, interest rates will rise, driving up the costs of borrowing, not only for the government, but for small business and families as well. As compound interest can aid growth, in reverse it multiplies debt with devastating effect. There is time, but the window of opportunity is closing.

In our first step toward *Compound Capitalism,* we must have money for compounding, and fulfilling that need requires that we find *Big Bills on the Sidewalk* to finance *Retirement Security Accounts, Retirement Healthcare Accounts* and *Lifetime Educational Support.*

Recall that the annual cost of the above three security benefits is $60 billion dollars; $32 for *Retirement Security Accounts*, $16 billion for *Retirement Healthcare Accounts* and $12 billion yearly toward *Lifetime Educational Support.* We will get this money from recurring annual savings.

Note, too, the fact that without *Compound Capitalism,* we are already on the heavy debt side of the ledger. The first step toward solvency must be dynamic. It needs large sums of new money quickly to be invested now, so that maximum time for compounding capital is built into the equation, and so that long-term debt can be subjected to the *Slaying the Dragon of Debt* process.

According to economist Paul Romer, there is a fixed cost for finding a set of new instructions (the essential details of a new concept) which is not restricted by the number of times or places the concept is used, so that the cost of each use goes down once the fixed cost is recovered. Economic journalist David Warsh puts it so well in *Knowledge and the Wealth of Nations*, his book featuring Dr. Romer's thoughts.

"Ideas, from intellectual property to the most basic research, could be copied practically without cost and be used by any number of persons at the same time. Innovations are another name for various 'new sets of instructions.'"

'New Sets of Instructions'

Cost differentials are a big idea—a very big idea! A new set of instructions. Cost differentials enable people who practice market capitalism to utilize these differentials to their advantage. Many already have. This is why *'Made in China,'* or *'Made in Bangladesh'* have replaced a former era's *'Made in USA'* shirt and ball cap labels.

'Competitive Advantage' is the term Harvard professor Michael Porter, a world expert, uses in over eighteen books he has written related to this topic, a much broader subject of study than just worker's wages. However, the fact that workers are paid much differently around the world, often for doing the same or similar tasks, is one of the recurring themes.

Now take a sidestep long enough to see that any savings, whether from reducing the societal cost of cancer, heart disease, diabetes, drug abuse, alcoholism, energy costs or some other burdensome cost, is a savings. A solution to any of these problems would save billions, because there is a cost differential between the current cost of a problem and the cost after the problem is cured. Solving problems creates savings.

Unintended Consequences

At one point in 2005, then editor Bill Emmott of *The Economist* raised the issue that solutions to one problem risked being shoved aside when they attempted to solve more problems than the one additionally addressed.

Our response then, and now, is that 'unintended consequences' are not always bad, or unable to be planned for, but can be considered *'serendipity'* when it turns out that more than one social good comes out of fortuitous turns of events related to an initial financial solution. We took Bill Emmott's challenge as an opportunity to look for examples in economics that would support the *'intended good consequences'* definition of *'unintended consequences.'* We found excellent support.

Nobel Laureate Amaryta Sen is famous for connecting the idea of development to the concept of freedom, a broad dual vision we applaud. He does not see any difference between the development of a person as contributing to freedom, or the development of a nation as leading to freedom.

Professor Sen then expands the view of the *'unintended but predictable consequence.'* His notion is that we may not directly intend a certain consequence in the sense of it being a first cause, but that there are predictable ancillary outcomes of both our acts and our political policy decisions. He puts it this way:

"It is a question of not being overwhelmed by the force of intention, and also of not ignoring the so-called side effects."

By this rationale, we can have what we intend and have the unintended consequences, too—and the unintended consequences can also be excellent! Reasoned social change should be examined carefully for both effects. This is not to suggest that things don't always go according to plan, although that is true, but that often they do.

The pie, so to speak, isn't of a fixed size, where the piece I eat diminishes the piece available to you. In a world where economic well-being has obviously grown throughout its breadth, its object is to assist all in gaining an ever larger share of a steadily growing pie. Bigger pies take more ingredients and one of the key ingredients is capital. Our plan provides that recipe, both to nations and to individuals, but with few and simple ingredients.

Economists like Dr. Sen might say decisions involving riddles like this, questions involving the preference rankings of less than all involved—should take notice of other relevant facts regarding dividing the pie, such as who is poorer than whom, who gains and who loses, how much comes from shifts in income and any other information, such as how the respective persons earned the particular shares of pie to which they feel entitled. We also care if the pie is earned—or looted from children. Why not give equal shares of just parts of the larger pies?

It's time to also look in detail at some of the *'unintended predictable consequences,'* those which, much like the *'invisible hand'* made famous by the father of modern economics, Adam Smith, lead to preferential consequences that lie outside the central theory or insight.

Largely credited for being the intellectual giant of democratic capitalism, outside academic circles Smith is not as well known for his book, *A Theory of Moral*

Sentiments, compared to his constantly read bible of capitalism, *Wealth of Nations*. It is important (particularly to non-economists) to be reminded that Smith's academic discipline was philosophy, not economics.

Smith published *A Theory of Moral Sentiments* seventeen years before his more universally known classic. It is often too easily forgotten that Adam Smith was never convinced of the inherent moral character of the powerful. Regarding moral sentiments, Smith cautioned us in 1759:

"The selfish and rapacious, are led by an invisible hand to advance the interest of society, which is gained without intending it, without knowing it."

With those few words, a concept that shaped a world was launched. Later, in his *Wealth of Nations*, Smith said:

"It is not from the benevolence of the butcher, the brewer, or the baker, that we expect our dinner, but from their regard to their own interest. We address ourselves, not to their humanity but to their self-love …"

In *Development as Freedom*, Nobel Laureate Amartya Sen again revisited Smith's butcher.

"The butcher sells bread to the consumer, not because he intends to promote the consumer's welfare, but because he wants to make money. Similarly, the baker and the brewer pursue their respective self-interests, but end up helping others. The consumer, in her turn, is not trying to promote the interests of the butcher or the baker or the brewer, but to pursue her own interest in buying meat or bread or beer. However, the butcher and the baker and the brewer benefit from the consumer's search for her own satisfaction. The individual, as Smith saw it, is led

by an invisible hand to promote an end which was no part of his intention."

Two other famous economists, Carl Menger and Friedrich Hayek, called Smith's insight fundamental to understanding that an unintended consequence need not be unpredictable. **This leads to the 'anticipated unintended consequence,' which, in fact, is predictable.**

It is the 'predictable and favorable unintended consequence' that is sought and found in *Compound Capitalism*. In this book we are examining the notion that there can be both far-reaching social consequences (greater emotional benefit, innovation, and sense of community) and economic consequences (greater growth, entrepreneurship and productivity) from the same action.

The fact that partially or wholly solving a problem issue, also solves a massive debt issue and a myriad of other social and economic issues is thus, a perfect example of "anticipated and favorable intended consequences."

Too much uninformed discussion has created the impression that only threatening and negative consequences are implied in the words 'unintended consequences,' that it always means something gone wrong. Such emotionalized rhetoric has included the sometime side-effects of prescription drugs, GM (Genetically Modified) foods, the greenhouse effect, food irradiation, technology, McDonald's, global integration and so on.

It is clear that anticipated, favorable, unintended consequences are not at all contrary to a tightly reasoned approaches to problem solving.

In Adam Smith's case, he also created a powerful metaphor of *'the invisible hand,'* a force that moves behind the scenes, to describe an elusive, creative and reciprocal element that was given birth as a part of his original insight. With Smith's powers of observation, this insight seemed inherently a part of life, born out by examining what he knew of the human condition and character.

No matter where real *Big Bills* money comes from to pay retirement security benefits or retirement income, healthcare and lifetime education support, Congress and the nation will face what are known as *'opportunity costs.'* These might range from being forced to postpone fixing one system in order to fund something else. It's always hard to have it all at once. Time moves on and every decision represents an opportunity gained or lost. Why wait, the golden opportunity is here for moving forward, even if one cure doesn't fix all ills?

Other Considerations

And Along Came the Dragon of Debt

The dragon was sleeping. In the first years of the new century no one yet knew how badly the money was going to be needed, or how much more would be needed. No one would have predicted that the debt would have grown by a staggering $10 trillion + dollars in just the last decade? We had not yet acknowledged an oncoming financial crunch, nor admitted to the overall seriousness of the long-term debt crisis. We couldn't get anyone to pick up *Big Bills Left on the Sidewalk* then…. Times have changed!

But the money is still there. You will more easily explain this huge cache of money to others knowing exactly how finding these Big Bills takes place.

"Give me somewhere to stand, and I will move the earth."

—Archimedes, Third Century B.C.E.

At the halls of Congress, Archimedes is knocking on the doors. He is shouting, *"Give me somewhere to stand, and I will move the earth!"* He thinks we have forgotten the power of levers; that imbalances, along with a well-placed fulcrum, are powerful forces indeed.

Since imbalances have their inherent powers, and even though Archimedes is not an elected representative, suppose Congress gave him an audience? One imbalance is the economic imbalance between nations, rich and poor. Nowhere are the differentials in financial leverage, what things cost and what people are paid, made more obvious than by this comparison. Not only are many nations poor, but their life expectancy is tragically as much as 30-40% less.

When reasonable solutions are at hand, not testing thoughtfully reasoned models can bring severe lost opportunity costs.

The United States can take full advantage of our leadership through public and private diplomacy. This response will strengthen our national image as a world leader and also increase our bargaining leverage when seeking cooperation in many vital matters.

Where will we find those first *Big Bills Left on the Sidewalk*, those very large piles of money just waiting to be capitalized to fund America's long term security needs— money, very real, but not yet picked up? We don't have an immediate cancer cure, or one to vastly increase our gas mileage, **but we do have terrific sources of *Big Bills Left on the Sidewalk.***

Chapter 11. Paying For It: Finding Big Bills on the Sidewalk

Just as a starter, let's consider The Heritage Foundation's carefully stated recommendations for cutting $343 billion from the Federal budget. We know well enough that every potential budget cut in even the best proposal is an invitation to political infighting, tooth and nail, to protect perceived vested interests. Even so, let's say that only a potential third of that, $114 billion, is retrievable. After all, Heritage is a well-respected source, recently having evenhandedly cooperated with the Brookings Institution on a joint tax-reform proposal. So, even if we nit-pick, lets call the potential savings $114 billion. **We will also continue the 'underestimate formula' on other already identified savings opportunities.**

Let's assume from now on a one-third value to one fourth for every dollar we pick up and lets call this first potential savings $114 billion.

CNBC's Squawk Box, with Becky Quick as host, recently examined the serious issue of tax evasion in a one-hour TV special, titled The American Tax Cheat. The program convincingly made the case that evasion was rampant and that $300 billion might be saved through more diligent enforcement. Three hundred billion is a lot of cheating. Once again, using our underestimated one-third formula, **think of a second realistic savings of $100 billion.**

Both Raymond Baker and Moises Niam wrote well reviewed books regarding illicit financial transfers. Baker's *Capitalism's Achilles Heel,* and Niam's *Illicit* point to as much as $600 billion annually—perhaps much more, and include financial issues such as tax havens, slavery, human trafficking, false invoices, money laundering, corruption, etc. (This list includes known U.S. product counterfeiting losses alone of as much as $200 billion.) **Think of the potential savings coming from illicit activity sources as $200 billion, 33% only valuation of $600 billions.**

Various agencies have listed the costs of illegal immigration to the U.S. as a cost of $30 billion annually to the Federal government and an additional $70 billion to State governments, a total of $100 billion. **Think of potential savings here as $33.3 billion annually.**

Food Stamp recipients have climbed from 26 million in 2007 to 44 million in 2011, with a cost increase from $33 billion to $77 billion, a $44 billion increase in just four years. A large portion of the total cost represents outright Food Stamp fraud, with everyone from prison inmates to lottery winners, duplicate cardholders, crooked retailers and lax rules administration being the villains. Saving just $32 billion of that would pay for the Retirement Income Security Accounts of Compound Capitalism. **Add $32 billion to Sidewalk finds.**

In fiscal year 2015 the Centers for Medicare & Medicaid Services (CMS)—the agency that administers Medicare and Medicaid—estimated that these programs made a total of over $43.3 billion in improper payments. It is instructive to note that the officially estimated $43.3 billion of Medicare and Medicaid fraud in a single year is more than sufficient to pay for the *Retirement Security Accounts* and *Lifetime Educational Support* programs proposed by *Compound Capitalism*. **Realistic savings might greater here at $23.3 billion.**

These few conservative savings opportunities alone represent a realistic expectation of $502.6 billion annual savings.

We can support *Compound Capitalism's Retirement Security Accounts, Retirement Healthcare Accounts*, and *Lifetime Educational Support* 8.38 times over each year, just from these discounted *Big Bills Left on the Sidewalk*, to say nothing of a whopping $442.6 billion in annual National Debt reduction.

"America's tax system is riddled with exemptions, deductions and credits that feed an industry of advisers but sap economic energy. Simply scrapping these distortions—in other words, broadening the base of taxation without any new taxes—could bring in some $1 trillion a year. Even though some of this would have to go in lowering marginal rates, it is a little like finding money behind the sofa cushions. The tax system would be simpler, fairer and more efficient."

—The Economist, January 20, 2010: America's budget deficit

Please note that we do not include this *Economist* estimate of $1 trillion dollars in potential savings. However, the source,*The Economist*, is certainly one to be given serious credence. You can decide if there are more *Big Bills* hidden on U.S. sidewalks. We think there are. We will show them.

Another potential we have not tried to add is the $600-$850 billion that respected news source Thompson Reuters claims is lost each year due to inefficient administration and unnecessary treatment and litigation costs of various medical issues. They quoted past OMB director, Peter Orszag, in a May 2009 interview with NPR:

"Estimates suggest that as much as $700 billion a year in healthcare costs do not improve health outcomes. They occur because we pay for more care rather than better care. We need to be moving towards a system in which doctors and hospitals have incentives to provide the care that makes you better, rather than the care that just results in more tests and more days in [the] hospital."

So, keep in mind that just these two areas of significant potential savings of $1.7 trillion dollars have not been included in our estimates of *Big Bills Left on the Sidewalk*. **We do not believe they have zero value, nor should you.**

We might also broaden the tax base (later), simplify the tax code (later), reduce the corporate rate from 35% to 25% (later) and reduce government 'duplication of effort.' **(Please note the State of California example of 'duplication of effort' in the Appendix.)**

As stated,later in *Compound Capitalism*, we will introduce a new savings and wealth creating sources associated with the reduction of corporate income taxes, expanding the tax code, expanding savings opportunity, better supporting innovation and other suggestions. In the meantime, We haven't exhausted the opportunities to gain more from what is already with us.

Chapter 12. More Big Bills Left on the Sidewalk

As we promised, there are plenty of *Big Bills*. Now we will consider the present U.S. high costs of mortality and economic related medical problems reported by Centers for Disease Control & Prevention. After this run-through we will address the top seven and costs, ruling out accidents. They are: 1. Heart Disease & Stroke, 2. Cancer, 3. Illicit Drug Use 4. Excessive Alcohol Use, 5. Diabetes 6. Obesity, and 7. Arthritis.

Compound Capitalism will invest annually across all seven areas, but again, **we will not attempt to determine a rate-of-return on that investment.** We will say that there will be a return. You will agree.

The Top Health & Medical Opportunities

Heart Disease, Stroke, Cancer, Drug Use and Abuse, Excessive Alcohol Use, Diabetes, Obesity and Arthritis are prime opportunities. In this grouping, 1,400,000 + lives are prematurely lost. We will allow you to place a loss value on that.

The total costs of just this short list is $1.593 trillions annually—yes, trillions! Medical science is a huge opportunity for saving both lives and money. We believe an annual investment by *Compound Capitalism* to be merited.

1. Heart Disease & Stroke: Death rates alone cannot describe the burden of heart disease and stroke. The cost of cardiovascular diseases in the United States, including health care expenditures and lost productivity from deaths

and disability, is estimated at more than $503 billion in 2010. As the U.S. population ages, the economic impact of cardiovascular diseases on our nation's health care system will become even greater.

2. Cancer: It is the second leading cause of death in the United States, exceeded only by heart disease. In 2007, more than 562,000 people died of cancer, and more than 1.45 million people had a diagnosis of cancer, according to United States Cancer Statistics: 1999–2007 Cancer Incidence and Mortality Data. The cost of cancer extends beyond the number of lives lost and new diagnoses each year. Cancer survivors, as well as their family members, friends and caregivers, may face physical, emotional, social and spiritual challenges as a result of their cancer diagnosis and treatment. The financial costs of cancer also are overwhelming. According to the National Institutes of Health, cancer cost the United States an estimated $263.8 billion in medical costs and lost productivity in 2010.

3. Drug Use and Abuse. Illicit narcotics inflict a societal cost of $400 billions annually and are the cause of 60,000+ lost lives. Alternate crop drug diplomacy with the six major producing nations and/or international protection enforcement of sovereign rights are prime savings opportunities, considering the vast cost differentials between producer and user nations.

4. Excessive Alcohol Use: Including binge and under-age drinking, it is the third leading preventable cause of death in the United States. This dangerous behavior is responsible for more than 79,000 deaths annually and a wide range of health and social problems. On average, for each death due to alcohol, an individual's life is cut short by 30 years. Excessive alcohol use also costs the United

States about $185 billion each year in health care and criminal justice expenses, as well as lost productivity.

5. Diabetes: Total costs (direct and indirect) of diabetes: $174 billion. Direct medical costs: $116 billion. Indirect costs (related to disability, work loss, premature death): $58 billion. People with diagnosed diabetes have medical expenditures that are about 2.3 times higher than medical expenditures for people without diabetes.

6. Obesity: In 2008, overall medical care costs related to obesity for U.S. adults were estimated to be as high as $147 billion. People who were obese had medical costs that were $1,429 higher than the cost for people of normal body weight. Obesity also has been linked with reduced worker productivity and chronic absence from work.

7. Arthritis: In 2003, the total cost of arthritis was $128 billion, which includes $81 billion in direct costs (medical) and $47 billion in indirect costs (lost earnings). Each year, arthritis results in 992,100 hospitalizations and 44 million outpatient visits.

Just seven of the top medical problems extract a cost of almost $1.6 trillion yearly. Solving problems is an American skill worth acquiring and repeating. Scientific, engineering and social are words not so far apart as one might think. Solving a medical problem is really not that different from solving an engineering or social problem. We want to chase debt-reducing solutions, where the profit in solving them is both obvious and substantial. It is usually preferable that problem solutions be profitable and that they create measurable savings. They are *Big Bills* additions to accounts, not deductions—new revenues, not debts.

We have no way to estimate the billions of potential savings that are the rewards for solving health and medical problems, but $1.6 trillion is a substantial sum and we are certain it demands sufficient attention. It obviously has a very significant opportunity value. We can help.

Solving problems is a beautiful way to make money, because the savings *"keep on keepin' on"*—year after year.

Compound Capitalism proposes to invest dollars annually from the initial $100 billion in yearly *Big Bills* savings to advance medical research in these areas. This is above the base investment for **RIS, RHS** and **LES**.

We would allocate the *Compound Capitalism* investment as follows:

Heart Disease & Stroke: $6 billion dollars annually

Cancer: $4 billion dollars annually

Excessive Alcohol Use: $2 billion dollars annually

Illicit Drug Use and Abuse: $1.5 billion dollars annually

Diabetes: $1.5 billion dollars annually

Obesity: $1 billion dollars annually

Arthritis: $1 billion dollars annually

***Compound Capitalism Assist*: $17 billion dollars annually**

Can we pick up Big Bills through our expertise in medical research and technology. We have already proven that we can. Average U.S. life expectancy has risen by 36 years since 1900.

Can we find more Big Bills Left on the Sidewalk, real money that we have failed to pick up?

Chapter 13. Even More Big Bills Left on the Sidewalk

Remember that cure equals savings. A solution to any major societal, medical, scientific, or applied technology opportunity would save billions, because there is a cost-differential between the current cost of having the problem and the cost after the problem is cured, all or in part. The cured or solved part creates a savings.

For purposes of *Compound Capitalism,* we are considering only those whole or partial savings opportunities that might significantly reduce governmental budgetary cost issues. We are not trying to measure potential savings of innovation developed and commercialized by private enterprise effort alone, only to measure those savings spin-off benefits also utilized by government. For example, a vast reduction in transportation energy costs would benefit government, industry and citizen consumers. We are also seeking opportunities to reduce or cut the cost of running government itself, for example, cutting defense spending procurement costs or simplifying tax codes.

If government were looking for a renewable energy source, why wouldn't it consider money saved? Government can create money without printing it simply by finding it in a place where previously it was like a vast untapped oil reserve, there all the time, but now politically obtainable, sort of an offshore money reserve.

What are we talking about? We are discussing a financial reserve that we can tap without risk of environmental damage. We are talking about the fact that Compound Capitalism can be financed without any new taxes, or cutting some legislatively favored budget!

First, in this chapter we will address several areas of potential Big Bills saving, with conservative estimates of knowing exactly how much might be saved from substantial or partial solutions applied to these areas of opportunity.

Later on, we will discuss widespread savings opportunities in such widespread areas as Defense, Tax Reform, Tax Evasion, Illicit Financial Flows, R&D, Patents and Innovation, Costs of Government, Health & Medicine, Biology, Biotechnology, Engineering & Manufacturing, Materials Science, Nanotechnology and others.

Following this discussion we will make recommendations concerning *Compound Capitalism* investment in selected areas of greatest potential, including considerations for investment in solving 'global' needs like malnourishment, malaria, immunization, etc. We are looking for savings of millions of lives, too.

Thou Shall Not Squander!

Any increases in tax revenues or revenue increases realized through improved economic growth, success of private enterprises, diplomacy, etc. will, of course, remain fully within the discretionary use of Congress.

Greater government revenues in the interim from the expected increase in the value of the dollar and subsequent increased foreign investment, or purchase of U.S. Treasury bills, will also be fully utilized as realized at the discretion of Congress. When the combination of events results in an absence of National Debt, Congress will have full use of all government receipts and savings.

In the interim, we recommend Congress be restricted from spending any savings derived from invested *Compound Capitalism* shareholder funds to promote new programs until such time as the National Debt is retired. As previously stated, interest on that debt is approaching $1 trillion annually. All interest reductions in the National Debt due to paying down principal will also be used to further and more quickly reduce debt.

There Are Still Plenty of *Big Bills Left on the Sidewalk*

It is clear to even the most casual observer of science that we are, as a recent editorial in the journal Bioscience notes, in the age of biology, biotechnology, genomics, nanotechnology, data and knowledge management, and much more: clearly, we are riding the crest of a profound era of science that is characterized by understanding the basic mechanisms of life, of natural systems, and the profound consequences of human endeavor in those systems.

Robert H. 'Rob' Carlson wrote *biology is technology*, (the lower case on the book's cover was his choice) published in 2010 by Harvard University Press and awarded the 2010 Engineering and Technology Book of the Year award. This is a short publisher's description:

Technology is a process and a body of knowledge as much as a collection of artifacts. Biology is no different—and we are just beginning to comprehend the challenges inherent in the next stage of biology as a human technology. It is this critical moment, with its wide-ranging implications, that Robert Carlson considers in *biology Is technology*. He offers a uniquely informed perspective on the endeavors that contribute to current progress in this area—the science of biological systems and the technology used to manipulate them.

In a number of case studies, Carlson demonstrates that the development of new mathematical, computational, and laboratory tools will facilitate the engineering of biological artifacts—up to and including organisms and ecosystems. Exploring how this will happen, with reference to past technological advances, he explains how objects are constructed virtually, tested using sophisticated mathematical models, and finally constructed in the real world. Many of the new discoveries will increase the human lifespan—we will live considerably longer.

And here is proof. On July 8, 2011, *The Wall Street Journal* ran a front-page article: *A Lifesaver, Custom Built in the Lab.*

"Doctors have replaced the cancer stricken windpipe of a patient with an organ made in a lab, a landmark achievement in regenerative medicine. The patient no longer has cancer and is expected to have a normal life expectancy," doctors said."

Almost any day's news contains some new story about a remarkable medical advance. The technology of the windpipe replacement above has potential applications for coronary arteries, the esophagus and ureter. And on the very next day, July 9, we read about the role of technology in the most recent of former Vice President Dick Cheney's recoveries from life-threatening heart disease. Such rapid increases in the power, availability, and application of technology and biotechnology raise obvious questions about who gets to use it and to what end or cost? It is of little wonder that healthcare costs reflect the rise of previously unavailable treatment options.

Carlson's thoughtful analysis offers rare insight into our choices about how to develop biological technologies and how these choices will determine the pace and effectiveness of innovation as a public good.

One of the fastest growing areas of science and technology is biology and biotechnology. *Compound Capitalism* plans to seize new opportunity in biological and agricultural technologies and proposes to invest $7.35 billion annually in new R&D in this area. Why?

A world of cheap food is gone. Institutions must change to meet the challenges of their times. Modern biotechnology compresses time and time frames—what were formerly eons are instants.

"The number of persons choosing to be malnourished, illiterate, lacking of basic possessions and drinkers of dirty water, and all at once, is fleetingly small."

The Economist, 7/31/10

Some areas of significant promise within this realm are both domestic and worldwide. One such opportunity is in agricultural biotechnology, particularly building nutritional elements, pest protection and draught resistance into food crops. Throughout the world, millions die from the direct and indirect results of malnutrition.

In particular, the way Dr. David Sands of Montana State University puts it:

"Science may be an endless pursuit, almost like a hobby, especially for those lucky enough to be doing science. However, for those 1-2 billion unlucky enough to be suffering from malnutrition, their suffering is endless, to a point. We may be on the verge of a 'nutritional revolution', where the empty calorie crops will be replaced with nutritious crops. Perhaps we should proceed rather quickly."

Dr. Sands has successfully selected for improved nutrition. The plant science group at Montana State is leading other institutions in the development of low glycemic new crop varieties of wheat, legumes and potatoes, all to reduce the unwanted high sugar contributions to heart disease, obesity and diabetes.

"Foods with high omega-3 content, low glycemic index and that are gluten free are widely recognized as important for health, and thus are desired by consumers."

Dr. Sands notes that by 2050 there will be 9 billion people to feed—two more India's so to speak, and that Africa's population will reach 2 billion, over half of them under age fifteen.

Disaster waits in the wings. Not only do we have to increase the food supply by as much as 70% by then, but as water, energy and fertilizers become more expensive, genetically modified crops will become more in need and more accepted for providing needed yields. "We need to add genius to genetics, we need many more young people engaged in agricultural science."

"As much as yields," Sands says, *"nutrition will become more essential in certain parts of the world. Bio-fortification in African foods, for example, will add iron, zinc, vitamin A, vitamin D and iodine to foods like wheat, maize, cassava beans and others."*

He laments that one-third of the world's plants suffer from the lack of micronutrients that fight off disease and help bodies grow healthily. Micronutrients include vitamins and minerals like folic acid, iron and vitamin A.

Not only are humans at risk, livestock must be healthily maintained. Meat is increasingly utilized in much greater quantities and probably needs to double. Meat requires eight times as much water as wheat. Drip-fed plants are on the increase as well.

The late Norman Borlaug referred to this as the *'gene revolution.'* At the 2011 World Economic Forum at Davos, leaders promised to do more "to promote a new vision for agriculture." We will build fertilizers into plants, with drought resistance as well. As soon as 2030, needs for water may increase by forty percent. All this while we know that only ten to twenty-five percent of usable land is still available for farming.

If one ever talked about the need for compound interest and compounding of efforts, now is the time. Moore's Law for plants is the galloping reduction of cost of the gene sequencing of plants. Even more genetics will be applied to wheat, rice and soybeans. In particular, we need to compound the number of people working on wheat.

There are Big Bills Left on the Sidewalk, lots of them, but we have to pick them up. One such sidewalk is represented by innovations, improvements and cost savings brought on by advancing science and technology. We must now consider the roles of innovation, entrepreneurs and R&D.

Chapter 14. More Big Bills: Innovation, Entrepreneurs and R&D

Innovation leads the way to economic growth.

Patents & Intellectual Property

It's time now to recall some words related to capitalism: opportunity, entrepreneur, innovation, incentive, reward and return.

America is still the leading producer of entrepreneurs, but the competition is getting tougher. Innovation is the fuel of entrepreneurs and of economic growth. In addition, theft of intellectual property, particularly huge cyber-theft from China, has been called *"The Great Brain Robbery."* In financial terms, estimates of China's cyber-theft exceed $350 billion dollar based on a federal estimate, though experts caution that the true number is impossible to know. It could actually be higher.

There is little question that mankind prospers from applied science and technology, particularly in the nation that leads the world both in developing and advancing technologies. Examples could fill a library. Not only has it been the wellspring of economic well-being, it has improved agriculture and nutrition, lengthened our life-spans and those of others and made it possible to send messages or dollars across the globe in fractions of seconds.

According to Michael Novak of the American Enterprise Institute, a precise capitalist insight is that innovation, creativity and entrepreneurship are more productive than rote labor. Therefore, the primary form of capital is *'mind.'*

The cause of the wealth of nations is *'mind.'* Capitalism is not constituted solely by private property, incentives, markets, free-trade, double-entry bookkeeping, rule-of-law or any other social techniques (though all of these are necessary elements), but rather by a social order favorable to alertness, inventiveness, discovery, creativity and the right to enjoy the fruits of one's own creativity.

Since technology is so much in our future's forefront, direct your inner vision to imagining the government enterprise as an entrepreneurial one that has divisions, sub-divisions, and yes—competitors. We have referred to government as being the business—the enterprise. After all, the objective of any government, as of any business, is to perpetuate itself and prosper.

Today the enterprise is facing a technological frontier that is well known, one in which America, the name of our business enterprise, is and has been the world leader. Our management and officers have already reached some basic agreements, at least in principle. We agree that we will ride the technology engine of growth into the new frontiers ahead. We agree that we must take a larger role in worldwide competition, making it both safe and prosperous to do business with others and for others to do business with us.

Goods and services from around the world fill our stores and fulfill our lives. We enjoy options as never before possible. Changing opportunities, responsibilities and world competition require that America continue its top position regarding innovation and entrepreneurship.

What lurks on the horizon to threaten this expanding cornucopia of benefits is the ability to better manage our resources, human, material and environmental; so that prosperity survives and is enjoyed, not only by more Americans, but also by those other nations.

Not too long ago, a popular musical jingle's lyrics were, *"I'd like to buy the world a Coke ..."* We think we have something much more lasting to share. America's best results will be gained by constantly reevaluating opportunities to reduce costs by both better management and more timely recognition of key areas for R&D investment, including support for U.S.-based advanced manufacturing.

Compound Capitalism's government, as a corporate entity interpretation, must allow for its officers to meet a range of needs that involve considerably more shareholder participation when possible, not only to meet the challenges of competition but also to carry on new functions. As with any business, or a government enterprise envisioned in a business suit, the overriding corporate objective is to perpetuate itself and to prosper.

It is not common to talk of governance as a beneficiary of its own programs, but this is the appropriate instance to make that claim. Instead of creating debt and liabilities of frightening size, the enacting of such a capitalistic restructuring enables government itself to become the beneficiary of more productive work efforts, not only from within ranks, but from without—from all allies.

Science and technology are not the areas of the greatest expertise for most elected officials. This is a problem demanding both recognition and action. We need to address a methodology to first make elected officials cognizant of the rush of scientific and technological advance, and then we must keep them at a high state of awareness.

In a market economy, government is expected to assign the responsibility to enact solutions to those who have earned the right to do so, either through singular competence or competitive superiority. But it isn't government itself that is expected to carry out the problem solving solutions. We are not in favor of government fingers in every pie and favor very careful selection of experts proved competent to act as trustworthy contractors.

William Baumol, who you have met earlier, is one of the champions of science and technology. He notes that entrepreneurs tend to cluster in places like Boston, Silicon Valley, Research Triangle Park, New York, Austin, San Diego and Los Angeles. Besides the occasional need for *'angel dust,'* the investments of families and others, *"What they need more than money,* Dr. Baumol says: *is an efficient patent system."*

Improving Innovation

In terms of creating both economic growth and new jobs, we need the success of entrepreneurs and innovators. In order to send the right messages to these creative people, we have to do a better job with both the time involved in the issuing of patents and their intellectual property protection. Even with legally sanctioned monopolies (like patents) lifespans are limited, not only by social choices, but by other necessities of stimulating new thought. Innovations can often be copied without the consent of the developer. Relative to human capital, *'intellectual property'* is much easier to copy.

The present patent office (USPTO) is a bottleneck of good intention, thrown into disorder and delay by far too little funding, too few expert staff, changing technology and

outside forces like 'patent trolls' adding to daily
administrative woes.

USPTO Director David Kappos told CBS News:

*"Every innovation comes through this agency on the way to
creating a business, whether it's the light bulb, whether it's the
laser, whether it's the iPod ..."*

*"We need to be the accelerant to Americans dreaming their
dreams, getting protection for them, putting them in the
marketplace, and succeeding or failing based on their merits."*

A twenty-five year IBM veteran, Director of the U.S. Patent
and Trademark Office, David Kappos and his successors
have a challenge, but little financial support. We hope to
change that.

Here are more quotes from Director Kappos that tell you
what it's like at USPTO.

*"In the technology field alone, consider the employment ripple
effect of Larry Page's 1998 patent for Google's search engine,
Steve Wozniak's 1979 patent for a microcomputer and Jack
Kilby's 1959 patent on the semiconductor integrated circuit."*

In 2010 there were 244,353 patents granted. That sounds
like a lot until you learn about the 'in box.' The 'in box' at
the U.S. Patent and Trademark Office is stuffed with
700,000 applications awaiting review. **Ultimately, only
four out of ten applications, or forty-two percent, are
approved. The current wait for a patent is, on average,
three years.**

"The backlog is indeed our biggest problem," Kappos concedes. *"It represents innovations trapped in this agency that otherwise could be creating jobs."*

Here's Director Kappos in Chicago speaking on a panel at the annual trade show of the Biotechnology Industry Organization.

"Hundreds of thousands of groundbreaking innovations that are sitting on the shelf literally waiting to be examined - jobs not being created, lifesaving drugs not going to the marketplace, companies not being funded, businesses not being formed - there's really not any good news in any of this."

And the news gets worse. The 1.2 million application backlog is because so many applications haven't even had preliminary review.

More than 700,000 of those 1.2 million applications in the pile haven't had so much as a preliminary examination. At an agency Kappos refers to as: *"our country's innovation agency'*—stifles economic advancement at exactly the time China is investing heavily in research and development, with both ideas of their own and those stolen from others

According to the World Intellectual Property Forum, China has the world's third busiest patent agency behind the U.S. and Japan, but it may soon overtake Japan.

An extensive *Milwaukee Journal-Sentinel* investigation revealed that in an effort to catch up with its paperwork, the agency rejected applications at an unprecedented 60% rate, including many that were later proved worthy of a patent.

"Highly innovative firms rely on timely patents to attract venture capital," Kappos said, adding that 76%of start-ups say their venture backers needed the validation of a patent to invest.

The potential companies are also unable to hire. Half of new jobs come from new companies in their first five years, according to figures cited by Gary Locke, then the U.S. Secretary of Commerce. *"New companies are established to monetize innovation … America may still be a world leader in key metrics of economic success—like levels of entrepreneurship, R&D investment and IT infrastructure – but a report last year from the Information Technology and Innovation Foundation concluded that no advanced economy has done less than the United States to improve its competitive position over the past decade."*

Knowledge is compounding so fast that the data accumulated in the past three years equals the volume of all previous recorded history. Think about that!

Compound Capitalism **proposes to support USPTO from the LES Account in the amount of $1 billion dollars annually, to be invested as follows:**

4000 New Inspectors & Technical Personnel: $400 million

100 New Attorneys & staff for consultation: $ 50 million

Investment in Cybersecurity: $100 million

Tracking Patent & Intellectual Theft: $100 million

Defending Against Patent Trolling: $100 million

Miscellaneous: $250 million

Compound Capitalism estimates that the payoff of this 'clear-the-decks of delay' investment will have a huge payoff in economic growth for America. How much we don't know, but it the fact that it matters is beyond dispute.

What commercial enterprise seems to do well is to isolate problems it thinks it can solve, then to figure out if solving it can make money. Perhaps government can learn something from this. Perhaps the top leaders in business and government should create more opportunities to share such thinking on a more regular and formal basis, so both parties might take each other's talents more seriously.

Small changes in a nation's growth rate create astonishing differences. Earlier on you met economist Paul Romer. He makes the point that when growth rates increase, they also compound. Romer calculates it for us:

"At 2.1% rate of growth per year, income per-capita in a nation can increase by a factor of 8 over 100 years, so if income per-capita were $30,000 per person, in 100 years that would be $240,000 per person. Now, imagine that you had a slightly higher growth rate. Suppose it was 2.6% instead of 2.1%. Then it would increase by a factor of 13 instead of 8, so you'd end up with $391,000 per person instead of $240.000. Small increments, even a half percent, accumulate into big differences in standards of living."

If you think Wal-Mart is old and very large, you are only half right. It didn't go public until 1972. Think about the fact, too, that of the 500 biggest companies in America in 1980, that only 202 were still in business just twenty years later. You will also be startled to learn that over five million small businesses start up every year in the U.S.

Opportunity-seeking is part of the American ideal.

While venture capital comes into play in entrepreneurship, it matters more in larger start-ups than in smaller ventures. We need to be developing brand new things, brand new ideas, brand new brand names.

In February 2011 testimony, Dr. John Holdren, then the Director of Science and Technology Policy, had this to say:

"President Obama, in his most recent State of the Union address, called on all of us to help create the American jobs and industries of the future by doing what this Nation does best – investing in the creativity and imagination of the American people. The President identified this time in history as our generation's Sputnik moment. And just as investments in science and engineering research and development (R&D) turned the original Sputnik moment into a Golden Age of American technological and economic dominance, so new investments in science, technology, and innovation (STI) will be the foundation for continued American leadership in the future. Targeted investments in the most promising frontiers of science, made in the context of responsible reductions in less productive endeavors, will fuel this trajectory and allow us, in the President's words, to "out-innovate, out-educate, and out-build the rest of the world."

'Sputnik moments' don't just happen. Saying something is not the same as having a plan to accomplish something. Golden Ages of anything not only need a plan, but they need the money to accomplish it. Unfortunately, Dr. Holdren didn't quite know where new money might come from. We do, and now you do, too.

Compound Capitalism proposes to increase the U.S budget proposals by $13.65 billion.

We propose to allocate that $13.65 billion as follows:

National Science Foundation—Increase $2.2 billion from *Compound Capitalism's Big Bills Savings Account.*

Advanced Technological Education (ATE) $26 million increase to educate technicians for high tech fields. This sum is subtracted from *Compound Capitalism's* LES (Lifetime Educational Support) annual budget of $12 billion.

Compound Capitalism's LES also proposes to increase the NIST (National Institute of Standards & Technology) budget by $100 million annually across areas germane to Advanced Manufacturing Technology, including laboratory research, health information technology, cyber-security, inter-operable smart grids and clean energy.

In addition, LES proposes to contribute $10 million to the Advanced Manufacturing Consortia program to develop plans for key research efforts.

LES proposes an annual contribution of $50 million to TIP, the Technology Innovation Program and $20 million annually to MEP, the Hollings Manufacturing Extension Partnership.

Compound Capitalism proposes a contribution to DOE, the Department of Energy, of $5 billion annually from its initial *Big Bills* $40 billions savings account.

Compound Capitalism would prohibit subsidizing electrical vehicles from this contribution. We believe that electric vehicles should merit their prices on competitive factors alone, without government support of consumer purchases. Products should compete on the basis of value and utility, not to satisfy any government giveaway. We would also repair roads and bridges before committing $53 billion to high-speed railways.

Compound Capitalism proposes a $450 million increase to ARPA-E, Advanced Research Projects-Energy, to grid technology, power electronics and energy storage.

Compound Capitalism proposes a contribution of $2 billion annually to support fundamental research through DOE's Office of Science in nanotechnology, advanced materials, high-end computing and other priority research.

Compound Capitalism proposes an annual contribution of $500 million to Department of Transportation (DOT) R&D, including NextGen Air Transportation System and research in highway construction materials improvements.

Compound Capitalism would offer an additional $35 million annually to the White House Office of Science and Technology Policy to broaden the science advisory function in order to improve the quality of science policy decision-making.

To other science and technology areas, to protect intellectual property and industrial technologies from criminal hacking and theft, *Compound Capitalism* proposes to allocate $1 billion annually to cybersecurity research and product development.

For the National Nanotechnology Initiative (NNI) *Compound Capitalism* would authorize an annual contribution of $500 million.

Regarding STEM education in Science, Technology, Engineering and Mathematics, we propose that **$2 billion dollars annually** be drawn from the *Compound Capitalism* LES budget to support Educate to Innovate and Change the Equation programs.

While we think it is necessary to develop highly effective STEM teachers, we believe that effort should concentrate on those who are already teachers and recognized competent on the basis of content knowledge of their subject area. We believe that social scientists don't make the best science and math teachers. In addition, we find it difficult to get teachers with strong content knowledge if they are not taught by teachers with strong content knowledge. So, first we have to test the teachers. To do that we need STEM applicants to be teachers who have passed a rigorous test. Then we need students who want to be content specialists, not merely holders of advanced degrees in General Education. They will need to be better paid than other starting teachers, because they are better qualified. That is sure to be a teacher's union issue, but it is placing a priority on measurable competence.

Too often, government has a number or objectives, but no real plan. We wonder who came up with the number of teachers needed as 100,000 and how many will be lost trying to net 100,000 and how long will that take? Will we need to train 500,000 to get a suitable 100,000? That is why we prefer for LES dollars to be spent only for advancing those already competent in a STEM subject area.

Compound Capitalism LES would also support an added annual effort to improve STEM education **by $500 million.** This money would develop STEM education for on-the-job training and adult education only.

Please note that $2.686 billions has been drawn from *Compound Capitalism's* (LES) Lifetime Educational Support fund balance of $11 billion. This leaves a temporary balance of $8.374 billion for K-12 production, vocational training, on-the-job training, technology training programs, books and other support materials, including joint industry/government program materials.

From that previous balance, $5 billion is now to be invested in developing new K-12 programs and materials. The balance in LES is now $3.374 billion.

Global Needs—Global Solutions

We also realize that some global needs have a strong moral component that may not always be best addressed only by market-profitability. In such cases, however, it is not impossible, nor undesirable, to add ethical and moral considerations. It isn't just cost/benefit analysis, although many needs do lend themselves to such measurements, even when human lives are at stake. And when lives are saved, human asset values are preserved. This is both the responsibility and opportunity cost of both governmental and non-governmental bodies—of belief systems. There are opportunities for government, business and NGOs to work together. Such cooperatives must be carefully chosen and strictly monitored, so that fund-granting bodies are not shamed by the lack of well-measured results rightfully expected of trustees.

Recently, the Copenhagen Consensus recommended spending $75 billion over four years ($18.75 billion annually) to attack a list of **global challenges.** All have a high return on investment, both social and financial.

The panel of eight economic experts included five Nobel Laureates. Copenhagen picked thirteen key areas needing global solutions. Among them are six that *Compound Capitalism* proposes to fund in their entirety, providing a stable source of annual outlay over the coming four years.

They are:

$60 million: Malnutrition supplements for children (Vitamin A & Zinc)
$286 million: Micro-nutrient fortification (iron and salt iodization)
$1 billion: Expanded immunization for children
$60 million: Bio-fortification
$27 million: Deworming and other nutrition programs at school
$798 million: Community based nutrition promotion

Compound Capitalism **Grant: $2.237 billion dollars**

From the *Compound Capitalism* $40 billion *Big Bills* fund, we would deduct this $2.237 annual sum for the next four years to insure a United States participation in combating Copenhagen's *'Global Crises'* Categories.

Foreign Aid and Free-Riders

This will set a strong example for OECD's other non-U.S. nations—nations benefiting from *Compound Capitalism Big Bills 'free-riding.'*

Potential Gains From Free-Riders

The best gains from *"free-riders"* are most likely to come from nations who decide to adopt their own versions of *Compound Capitalism*. As we have stated, "recipes" are 'non-rival goods' that can be used in other places. *Compound Capitalism* can be adopted elsewhere.

Nations build reputations on leadership, not 'free-riding.' Europe has long been protected under an American security blanket since the start of the Cold War. The blanket is still there—well after the threat has lessened considerably. America's NATO 'free-riders' do not fully plug in to heat their share of the blanket by their money, energy or effort. They tend to hog the blanket. Britain and France currently spend less than half the almost 5% percent of GDP spent by the U.S. The rest of NATO gives even less, Germany at 1.15%, Italy at 0.91% and Spain at 0.69%.

A good current example is the predominance of U.S. cost was Libya, a clear NATO past defense interest. Speaking in the past, U.S. Defense Secretary Robert Gates then warned our European allies in NATO that freeloading on America's outsized military-might cannot guarantee their security forever, or even in the near term, which Gates said could soon turn *"dismal"* for the alliance.

"When the going gets tough the tough get going." There are many *Big Bills Left on the Sidewalk.*

From the *Compound Capitalism's Big Bills Savings*, we have now drawn an added $40 billion annually, making the total expenditures from that fund $100 billion. That includes $32 billion for Retirement Security Accounts,

$16 billion for Retirement Healthcare Accounts, and $12 billion for Lifetime Educational Support.

Can Citizen Shareholders Share in U.S. Government-Funded R&D?

We don't know, but we hope so.

A short and obvious political answer now regularly given is that we already do share in returns, but our question relates to actual ownership interests, the direct sharing of growth and dividend revenues, not sharing only in the sense of enjoying the benefits of use. We are looking to find more opportunity for citizens to expand their shareholding interests. We want to enhance capitalist citizenship, not just government. It was all taxpayer money that was used.

We believe that government enterprise funded R&D should seek, wherever possible, to share shareholder investments with their investors. Our hope in recommending this concept for consideration is the knowledge that people are more responsive and supportive of ventures in which they have a stake. If taxpayers could become more aware of what government invests in, and also had a more personal way to be associated with that investment, instinct tells us that citizens would subsequently be more supportive of government as a venture capitalist or as a financial supporter of private venture capitalists. What happens when citizens have skin-in-the-game?

We keep reminding you that the enterprise (the institution of government) gets all of its revenue from citizens—that in one form or another, government is merely a trustee for other people's money. Therefore, when the institutional enterprise invests in specific R&D with shareholder funds, the shareholder might be justified to own part of that investment. Exactly how that could best occur needs considerable discussion and perhaps should only apply to large-scale investment—perhaps apply to only R&D expenditures over a certain dollar figure or to a clearly new enterprise. One concept is that every large Federal R&D project might begin with a two to five percent stake already owned by a 'Citizen Debt Reduction Agency,' or some such name, and that the percentage allocated up-front followed the innovation to getting a patent or license and to either commercialization or failure to commercialize. In that way, citizens might feel that their government was making wise investments and that they were direct beneficiaries. The *'skin-in-the-game'* concept is that, the more strongly shareholders view their enterprise, the more involved they are. Perhaps this would apply only to start-ups based on an innovation, as one could not yet own a percentage of a large, established corporate entity, probably only in a separate spin-off. (please see Corporate Tax Reform section) Here's a recent example of the kind of project in which citizens might share.

The MIT D-Series

A recent news item that illustrates this point was the NASA investment of $2.1 million made to MIT for designing a new type of transport aircraft, with the Boeing B737-800 as a model platform.

What that starting point became, under Dr. Mark Drela at MIT, is a D-series of about the same size, but whose D8.1 version could be built now with current materials and save 49% percent in fuel costs. The D8.5 version would be built from future composite materials not yet available, and would have to wait until 2035 to be ready. It would burn an incredible 71% less fuel. Since the fuel savings from either version would be in the multi-billions of dollars, it raises the question as to whether or not, or how the citizen stockholder might benefit directly, rather than indirectly through lower airfares? Certainly the military cost of fuel would be a direct reduction for the Defense budget. Should this savings reduce the National Debt? We are suggesting that at a minimum, budgetary savings at the government level, gained through the benefit of citizen dollar investments, might be the kind of future savings opportunity that venture hawks would seek out.

Citizen tax revenue investments in joint government and/ or university research and development might also gain from the savings or commercial success of that individual taxpayer (shareholder) investment in a similar way.

Chapter 15. Immigration

Shareholding aspects of *Compound Capitalism* have been justly earned by prior and future legal persons, either by contributions already made or by future contributions logically anticipated. With assets to be accrued per individual equal to almost one million dollars by retirement age 67, ($615,000) and with another ($307,500) retirement healthcare security and lifetime educational support, admission by illegal means to asset ownership by criminal entry creates too high a human temptation to secure illegal admission. We must also not restrict our own citizen's right to innovate and grow by fear of envy or worse on the part of others.

With all the many benefits already suggested by *Compound Capitalism* that will raise both opportunity, financial growth, individual education, incomes, heath benefits—all increases over the present, one must also recognize that standards for legal immigration must be raised and illegal immigration prohibited. People being people, an America gaining the citizen benefits of shared capitalism is an almost an invitation to violate our borders. To the merely greedy, those seeking freebie or merely poor people or genuine asylum seekers, the newly gained advantages of citizenship will be coveted. In addition, at a time when applicants cannot be verified as worthy or even non-violent or favoring of religion based government, rules for obtaining citizenship must be completely changed. *Compound Capitalism* must protect its own new contractural relationship with its own legal citizenry, or it will fail.

Borders sometimes illustrate the vast differences between countries. Borders will be changed by what we propose—so will relationships with our own citizens. Some borders are relatively open, others tightly sealed. There are numerous examples that leave little doubt regarding how much government borders matter. Look at the contrasts between Hong Kong, South Korea, Taiwan and China during the infamous famine era of Mao vs. the more modern China; recently awakened to emulate better aspects of the same near neighbors. Look too, at the volatile sensitivities between North Korea and South Korea or India and Pakistan, just to give examples.

Consider the surprising contrasts between the United States and Mexico, with only the meandering Rio Grande making up much of the border. Think of fences, tunnels. Today's Mexico occupied the same area long before there was a Mexico or a United States. Despite first occupancy, it is unquestionably apparent that the differences in economic well-being and human capital development are much better organized by the American newcomers to the North.

Looking southward, directly across the Rio Grande from El Paso is Ciudad Juarez. Of last year's total 15,000 drug gang murders throughout Mexico, that city alone suffered 3,000+ killings.

Yes, there are U.S. plants in Mexico, and trade agreements. But Mexico is also torn by an ongoing tornado of corruption, criminality and a loss of national control. Making border relations even more difficult are the 50+ tons of pure heroin sent to the U.S. from Mexico's Guerrero State mountain region in the Sierra Madre del Sur. Mexico is the transit zone not only for home-grown narcotics, but also for those of Colombia, Bolivia and Peru. A kilo of cocaine wholesale is $12,500 and up, depending on the level of impurities—250-350 tons head yearly to the U.S.

The angry winds are blowing. This is not accidental or bad luck. A newer grim result of Mexico's epidemic is the deadly spread of gang warfare throughout Central America's borders, a contagious disease now creeping both north and south. According to the U.S. Department of Justice 2010 report, the Central American cartels are a growing threat.

Southern Command Chief, Air Force General Douglas Fraser, puts it this way: *"... deadliest zone in the world outside Iraq and Afghanistan."*

In the U.S., the homicide rate is 6.4 per 100,000. In Honduras it's 77.5, El Salvador 64.8, Guatemala 46.5 and Mexico 18.0. If conditions worsen, more illegal immigration will follow. We will pay a high price for easy Central American immigration.

Borders are a crucial element in revitalizing American capitalism through common shareholding at either birth or naturalization. Borders are now much more critical. It is now impossible to look at the differences between borders without examining the role of immigration vis-à-vis our own well-being under *Compound Capitalism.*

Present interpretations of the 14th Amendment grant citizenship to all those born within U.S. territories, without regard of having a fetus arrive via a pregnant illegal entrant or being born to an illegal immigrant already within a U.S. boundary.

Since substantial built-in future financial security mechanisms are to be set in place by vastly improved retirement, health and educational security end results, gaining access to that must be restricted to families who have already arrived in America legally, or have become legal through naturalization. Otherwise, we are inviting thieves, or those seeking a handout, not persons coming as contributing guests.

Although the 14th Amendment is subject to more restrictive interpretation, it must now be stated again more clearly, without ambiguity. Such a beneficial skin-in-the-game citizen circumstance in the U.S. almost surely will open the floodgates to illegal financial 'free-riding' of a destructive nature. In order to protect the benefits offered by *Compound Capitalism,* we must not sacrifice our own best human resources and their futures to unlawful entry.

Logical reasoning also hastens a much more practical reality, that the rapidly changing United States does indeed need many new immigrants, but now those with different skill qualifications and educational attainments from generations past. The days of '40 acres and a mule' are are long past.

Workers Wanted is a needed sign that asks boldly for new foreign workers. It is an employment opportunity. We might easily seek as many as 2,000,000 immigrants per year, allocated as follows:

Temporary Workers

Starting with temporary workers, we would be open to as many as 500,000 to fill advertised job opportunities, probably mostly in agriculture and jobs requiring more physical than formal intellectual attainment. This group would enter and exit as needed by U.S. employers and for such time periods as contracted for by employers, but no longer. Immigration and Customs Enforcement (ICE) should be concentrating on employment verification, criminal acts and national security.

Employment verification should be mandatory, not voluntary. These persons would be issued biometric iris-scan ID cards that would clearly designate them as temporary work visitors, not as green card or H-IB visas. Employers would verify all hires and terminations.H-IB Visas

The second category would be H-IB visas for highly skilled individuals, persons needed for future innovation and entrepreneurship, open to as many as 300,000. H-IB employer sponsored immigration petitions allow skilled foreign workers to be employed from three to six years by their corporate sponsors. Between 1995-2005, 25% of the high tech start-ups in the U.S. had at least one immigrant as a key founder. These companies alone have created 450,000 jobs. ISCIS might also consider fee reductions to facilitate entry, now as much as $2,000 on some petitions.

Green Card Applicants

The third category, **1,000,000 each year,** would be for Green Card applicants, those desiring to become citizens fully assimilated into American society.

However, Green Card rules would change significantly. For example, current rules permit those admitted legally to extend emigration opportunity to family members in home countries. **That practice would cease abruptly, particularly as older relatives constitute long-term retirement and healthcare security risks that taxpayers can no longer afford.** The kinds of immigrants favored would be younger, and those already literate in their own languages, with added preference given to those also literate in English. **An absolute prerequisite would be to test literacy in reading and writing in the proposed immigrant's own language.** Rosetta Stone testing, of a sort, but applied in reverse. **Applicants must demonstrate a present competence level, as requirements for future citizens must be higher than in the past.**

Students

The final group of immigrants are foreign students, which might total approximately 400,000 annually, split almost in two between undergraduate and graduate students, a cumulative potential for as many as one million in the country at a given time. These students contribute as much as $18 billion to the American economy. **(More than enough to pay for RHA.)** At present, students from India and China account for 45% of foreign students in U.S. graduate schools. Throughout America, foreign students make up ten percent of the grad school enrollment.

Illegal Residents

Regarding the estimated 11 million illegal immigrants already in the U.S., it is estimated that over 350,000 infants are born into this grouping annually. The negative economics this entails needs to be addressed sensibly.

Our intent is that illegal immigrant parents be required to compensate the U.S. Treasury over a suitable period of time to avoid deportation and attain their own citizen naturalization. The aim should be that all permanent residents be citizens.

We suggest an illegal head-of-household-only rate of $1,000 annually for a period of twelve years, or $12,000— or sooner if earlier naturalization is affordable and desired. Illegal immigrant parents would have 180 days to register. **Those discovered afterwards would be deported.** There should no longer be judicial review of cases in which the illegal has already broken the law—but to clear the slate, there is a no-nonsense review, conform, pay up or ship out. There should no longer be non-citizens other than diplomats, media and legal visitors. America does not need residents, **we want talented citizens.**

This offer would also be combined with requiring illegal parents to meet U.S. standards for naturalization and to acquire it within that same twelve-year period. The sooner they achieve naturalization the better, **for only at naturalization would their own retirement security and long term health security accounts be invested and begin to earn interest**. Suffice to say, that only those enrolled at birth will achieve the full amounts in both security accounts.

The intention, of course, beyond the protection of legal citizen rights, is to encourage a more educationally advanced level of immigrant, and to deny any further exploitation of *'birthright citizenship'* to game the system.

Asylum Seekers and National Security

As to requests for asylum, or requests on other humanitarian grounds, new standards would apply regarding whether or not such persons were likely to be future liabilities rather than contributors. We would hope that United States Citizenship and Immigration Services (ICIS) experts in immigration matters would welcome the opportunity to set appropriate guidelines.

With the advent of pre-invested future security funds at stake, along with the need for vigilance against terror or illegal actions, Americans will realize that the only way to protect the heritable gains for themselves and offspring will be to establish solid identity protection systems that prevent unauthorized institutions or individuals from making criminal use of citizen supported assets and value systems.

At a tense time when we need to know who comes to our shores with the intent to cause harm, we also need to examine those of more innocent intent; those who desire entry for purely human reasons. We cannot deny that the aim of most would be to enjoy the best that the best has to offer, except that the best cannot freely offer it to everyone and long remain the best. We need standards.

The advent of nations and borders has precluded all claims to unrestricted freedom of movement. Nobody likes not being invited to the world's best party, of course, but we have just fully invited our own citizens to *Compound Capitalism* for the first time. What we can do and have done today is to create a non-rival model of shareholder capitalism and governance that may be copied by any nation that covets the recipe.

Americans need not be ashamed of success. What we have gained to date is not something others have lost, but a result that has been earned by those who have it. The person who watches TV in a foreign nation and is envious of America is watching a success story, not a mugging.

Compound Capitalism is scaleable to many sizes of nations and internal revenues and would provide dramatic citizen benefits, if applied there tomorrow.

In a nation like Nigeria, for example, or others where natural resources like oil are confiscated regularly by autocrats, the *Compound Capitalism* model would change life for its citizens. It is estimated that from 1960-1999 Nigerian officials stole or wasted $440 billion in public monies, mostly oil revenues. Today it spends 3% of its budget on education and 1% on health. Because Nigeria or others won't benefit their own citizens, when resources to do so are available, is not a viable argument that America should favor that nation's immigrants. Nations must do their rule-of-law reforming from within—there is no legitimacy to a borderless world and no legitimate onus placed upon success.

Chapter 16. Corporate Tax Reduction—The Corporate Two-Cents Worth

There has been constant effort toward reducing U.S. corporate tax rates to a more competitive worldwide rate, hopefully 25% rather than 35%. There is little question that U.S. corporations would be better able to compete on a more level playing field. We should not penalize our own enterprises.

But what if citizens shared in the corporate tax reduction benefits that are hoped for by every U.S. based corporation? How? What if the citizen and the government both shared from reductions of corporate taxes to more internationally competitive rates?

Discussion has not been initiated to present government with an immediate incentive to reward corporate goals for growth. We suggest an exchange of benefits and assets between governing America and producing America.

In exchange for a permanent corporate tax reduction to 25% or even a 20% rate, U.S. corporations agree to transfer 2% of all classes of stock to a *U.S. Government Asset Trust.* This would transfer approximately $900 billion in market value to that trust. This would not be a *'managed'* trust in the normal investment trust sense, since every corporation's contribution is equal. In addition, all new incorporations would also contribute 2% of their stock to the *Government Asset Trust.* **States in which corporation's are incorporated would not be permitted to apply the same concept in an attempt to gain asset income leverage.**

It's a purely *"I'll scratch your back if you'll scratch mine"* exchange, but with the benefit that government will gain wealth producing and growing assets to better protect against debt growth and shrinking dollar values.

Although an innovation, we consider it more naturally, evolutionary in nature, assuming on our part that having historically neglected to do this in the past is more a political shortsighted mental slip-up that failed to value the concept of a participating and shared form of capitalism, where all parties have a skin-in-the-game ownership interests in the government enterprise.

Whatever the decision, we encourage debate on this proposed exchange of obvious benefits.

Chapter 17. The Citizen Two-Cents Worth: The 2% Skin-In-The-Game Tax

We have outlined in detail a number of sidewalks where *Big Bills* have been left and are available. If you didn't like any of the savings opportunities presented, here's one certain to raise the needed funding for *Compound Capitalism* and presented in the same sense of shareholding as throughout the book. All citizens are shareholders. **All have skin-in-the- game.**

If there were a shared taxpaying gene, government would have a monopoly on its conditions of inheritance. Since government does have a monopoly on setting the taxpaying aspect of our genes, we must take care to preserve those aspects of the self that are our own shareholders monopoly. These include our opinions, our desires, and to a large extent, our accomplishments. When we are at our youngest, these aspects have yet to find full expression, but the potential of great productivity is within each of us. Why not formalize a sharing relationship?

If the same government with a monopoly on taxing had the opportunity to choose the kind of citizen it wants, rather than the ones it gets, that monopoly would immediately increase in value. In a situation in which the Nation has a choice, it would not opt in advance for under-achievers nor indiscriminately make large commitments to those inclined more to being beneficiaries than contributors. In fact, in the degree to which citizen's potential for productivity is increased, such increases would enable a consistently less forceful exercise of the government taxing monopoly.

Despite that, this monopoly power does not impact all of us. **Other than payroll withholding taxes, that benefit only the payees, we have a system in which at any given time, 51% of the citizens of our republic make no income-tax contribution to support the general needs of the community. None!** Either certain incomes are considered too low, or they qualify for enough credits, deductions and exemptions to eliminate their liability. According to projections by the Tax Policy Center, a Washington research organization, the top 10% percent of taxpayers pay 72% of the taxes. It's hard to make the case that the rich don't pay a fair share. The Federal income tax is the government's largest source of revenue, raising more than $1.3 trillion—from a record $3.25 trillion in Federal tax receipts.

As you walk down any street, you might easily visualize that one out of every two passers-by pays no income taxes. How does it make you feel to be carrying the load of someone else? Do you ever think about it? Do you ever think if someone is carrying your load, not the former thought?

In contrast, how would it make you feel about your citizenship status if everyone, each within their capacity to do so, was making themselves productive, not drawing down on scarce resources, but also contributing enough to the tax base to have skin-in-the-game? If you say that arrangement would make you feel better, you should like this option. It gives government the right to ask you to purchase a small piece of your own and your children's future well-being by paying a 2% income tax on any gross income you receive, despite the fact that the source of that income may be your government. That would apply to all citizens—2% would be the lowest bracket, someone making $10,000 would pay $200.

This 2% tax, by itself, could purchase the productivity shareholder *'paper'* of *Compound Capitalism* even if some other source of *Big Bills* already found was not utilized. It might also be in the magnitude of $250 billion annually. If for no other use, proceeds should be used to reduce the National Debt, a benefit for all.

When government accepts your human capital asset in advance, it acknowledges the existence of a contractual and collateralized relationship, a *Compound Capitalism* shareholding interest created on your behalf. Your fellow citizens have arranged for this in return for your lifetime loyalty and willingness to pledge a financial and spiritual allegiance to the same fellow citizens, also represented by your government. For this, you get an opportunity guaranteed for life as a contributor to the productivity of the entire community, represented by your elected fellow citizens as well. It's a terrific feel-good way to get your two-cents worth!

Compound Capitalism Conclusions:

Hope fits all sizes—and all ages.

Okay America, we've given you the future and the present.
Attend the performance!

**Einstein had it right! The true miracle of compound
interest is that investing in retirement income and health
security funding at birth for 268,000,000 Americans over
the next 67 years of each life has not cost anything, not a
cent.**

If each citizen born in the next 67 years had lived till
retirement age 67, not even counting how many years they
live after 67; the total just at 67 between both accounts
would be $245,220,000,000,000! That's $245 trillion dollars
—without the $220 extra billions.

**Perhaps you don't often see a "trillion" on paper? If you
want to check the math, multiply 268,000,000 million
Americans times $922,000 ($615,000 in Retirement
Security Accounts and $307,000 in Retirement Healthcare
Accounts). We also easily lose sight of the fact that the
Big Bills are 'found money' from the start; so don't forget
we got it free from finding new money and just couldn't
touch it till retirement.**

The most important fact of our conclusion is that the U.S.
has the financial capability to pick up many more *Big Bills
Left on the Sidewalk* than are required by *Compound
Capitalism's* three long-term security programs, RSA, RHA
and LES—many times more!

We have considered as much as $3 trillion dollars annually that might be on sidewalks we have overlooked beyond the $500 billions annually we have declared solid. Three trillion dollars is 3,000 billions. **That could pay the national debt in less than two presidential terms.**

A good friend once sent me this insight that seems appropriate here: *"Even though we are living much longer and face an uncertain financial future, when you are dead, you won't even know that you are dead. It's a pain felt only by others. It's the same result when you are stupid."* **Why should we transfer pain to our nation and our fellow citizens when we can spare them now—share future successes rather than failures? Why be stupid?**

The three new accounts (RSA, RHA and LES) solutions ask for $60 billion from those potential $3,000 trillion (that's 30,000 billions) savings. We have located reliable sources for over $500 billion *Big Bills Left on the Sidewalk* annually, and presented others so that you could see for yourself that much greater savings are all around us—most gained through nothing more than better management—some by better ideas. There are many reasons for you to become an interested party and a skin-ind-the-game shareholding capitalist. The best reason is the magic of compound interest.

Peggy Noonan, writing for the Wall Street Journal was blunt in a recent article headline: *Word of the Decade, 'Unsustainable.'*

We sought a new way to release the *'latent'* energy represented in the unused productivity inherent in newborn and new citizens, to create a seamless transition to responsible and inspired citizenship. Like cracking the atom, we needed a transformation process that would allow us to split that atom, disengaging a real property asset from its inherent energy potential. Initially, we did this because we needed to solve the existing but flawed social contracts, Social Security and Medicare/Medicaid; failed systems headed for bankruptcy. In the process we discovered we had solved much more than was intended, one of those marvelous moments of serendipity that is discovery's reward. The fact that we got to do so much more in the problem solving process has something to do with the quality of the solution and everything to do with challenge creating opportunity.

If such positive results are possible, what should we think about those individuals who can change all human outlooks for the better, but don't?

Today, the enterprise of governance is facing a financial and technological frontier that is well known, one in which America, the name of our *'City on a hill'* enterprise, is and has been the world leader. The leader on the hill is looking over a steep cliff. Our managers and officers have already seen this view and have reached consensus.

There has been general agreement that more citizens must be provided with a different and better education so that functioning in a technological world is both easier and more productive. That's why all the enterprise's officers and management keep stressing the need for education, because it helps both the customer and the business.

Also, we agree that in order to meet challenges, most yet unknown, we need to make better use of our resources; intellectual, physical and economic. Within this broad framework, we know that if we are to lead, we have to make better use of each resource, not just a few and not just in the aggregate, but one resource at a time. We

know that we cannot promote the idea of prosperity at home if we allow too many citizens to be dissatisfied.

We may be surprised to relearn, although it often seems otherwise, that in modern business thinking, the customers rule the business; that the business will risk failure if, over an extended period of time, it neglects to provide satisfaction regarding products and services. One way or another, customers always vote.

Citizen stockholders, of course, continue to hold management elections, either re-electing incumbent members or choosing leadership more appropriate to solutions. The citizen stockholders will then have self-created a newer, more streamlined management firm to meet the challenges of the rapidly changing world, an interconnected world where compounding interests in science, technology, information and complexity are the rule, not the exception. In demanding the type of organization needed, the citizen stockholders have granted the firm the responsibility not only to debate what is needed in the short term, but also to address vital changes needed for the future.

Is there any inconsistent goal expressed when a political leader tries to employ strategies that enhance greater social, economic or moral results for his nation? In short, why do we say that long-term planning, assisted by leaders we elect is a better choice than planning for just the next election cycle, when it generally seems not only right, but necessary for companies in which we invest to do that very thing—plan for the future? And in fact, when we find they don't address pressing issues by rational planning, we then go hunting for new CEOs.

Different intellectual capacity inhabits each mind. There are plenty of differences in humans, some visible—more that are not. These natural variables separate individuals from each other and even from their cultures. So, how can minds be compared? John Nash, the man honored in the film, *A Beautiful Mind*, came from a poor region of West Virginia. Good minds are everywhere. Our gifts, while shared in degree, differ in both quantity and quality and are inequalities of fact, not of philosophy. They acclaim diversity, not refute it. The differences do not constitute rights of separation, only rights of use. They are gifts, not the preferences of heaven.

Inequalities can lead to greater difficulty, greater opportunity or greater obligation. Certainly social and biological differences will continue to play their part. More than any other striving, each mind seeks dignity. In gaining dignity, it is not that differences are denied, but that similarity of worth is affirmed.

At the same time we value human capital differences, we can't have job opportunities and societal or intellectual drop outs to fill them. Unfulfilled opportunity not only diminishes the productivity of society, but also blemishes the beauty of liberty. In addition to solving the Social Security and retirement healthcare financing problems, *Compound Capitalism* strikes a mighty blow on the side of human spiritual capital, not an insignificant unintended consequence. It provides an environment conducive to enhancing cooperative opportunity—of adding living substance to what are usually only empty words.

Why would government (remember that government is you and me) do this? First, we need to solve the retirement security and healthcare issues one way or another. Do we expect to give something to the nation it

wouldn't get otherwise? Yes! The answer to the last question also answers the first, because the collective 'We', is the people and what 'We' expect is, that by assuring aspects of citizen's futures at birth, you in return will be a more productive citizen in every regard throughout the whole of the lives of 'Us' together. It is a matter of reasoned communal belief.

One of those reasoned beliefs is that the national saving rate needs to rise to help fund future economic growth. Changing to an asset based investment trust vastly increases the nation's savings rate. Composite savings will accrue from strengthening both our national savings rate and, in consequence, the dollar and thus increase its desirability as a world currency.

Most people know there are things more important than money. That knowledge does not make them wish to be poor. And it is not so much money itself that is valuable, that always helps, but it is money strategically arranged for use that is often more important than its quantity. It's that *'truth,'* too, that we have tried to employ in our solution—to put money to work when it does the most good and before it's actually needed. Man doesn't always need more money, but money when it's needed most.

The community *'We'* are convinced that your knowing there is a brighter rainbow for the individual *'you,'* will cause you to be more optimistic, healthier and a better citizen. We figure *'We'* will gain in every regard, and that less money will be needed to take care of things that go wrong when people are not happy or do not have a sense of dignity. We have done all this to support the idea of democratic capitalism, asset building, accomplishment and community. We also believe that the rule-of-law is strengthened when everyone owns real property, that when widespread respect for ownership of property is established, in fact as well as in principle, that opportunity for all has been increased.

Our young must be able to do well. Only when they do well can they do that which is good. We don't want our young to think that their life's fortune depends upon 'heads or tails,' but that the pursuit of happiness is a term intended to have substance, not an unfulfilled promise. Ours is a promise with real meat on the bones. It can't solve everything, however.

An intended spirit of human dignity surrounds enhanced capitalism. It is not based on status at birth, but that each one of us is born to make a contribution to the future of our nation. We will do this naturally, sometimes whether we want to or not, just by being us, by being born, perhaps serving our nation otherwise. No matter what happens, we will make some productive contribution, most certainly by being taxpayers, but in many other ways, too, unknown to us at birth. And serving well is not an entirely unselfish, altruistic act on anyone's part. That's because we know that saving for the future gives all Americans a better chance, which saves each one of us both tax dollars and distress over the long haul. We cannot waste the future's resources, our children's talent or their money long before their future arrives.

The equality part—we will be expected to work at on our own. It is not that we will never again walk life's uncertain tightrope, but that one can walk with much greater confidence when looking at a strong safety net below, particularly when we own the net. Unlike the current net, which makes no guarantee and has no property value, we intend to provide a safety net with income guarantees and property values and health security support that both accumulate tax-free and are heritable. Real property promotes confidence, purpose and dignity.

Perhaps no plan does away with envy—thinking we each can have everything we want and are also entitled to it. That is not capitalism. It does, however, create a future that enables each of us to use whatever talents we have in giving life our very best shot. That's because each new person welcomed into the opportunities outlined will end up pretty well off financially.

We believe that lifetime productivity should be the worthy precursor to both consumption and the building of inheritable wealth. We do not take the narrow view that freedom and independence require only the continued ability for consumption, but that inheritable capital compliments and continues the cycle of productivity and that financial worth promotes feelings of self-worth.

It is one thing to reward productivity potential, which is yet unrealized, but it should not be necessary to repeat that cycle again and again after productivity has been rewarded at birth.

We work for government all our lives, but for other specific employers, the time has become vastly shortened. According to the U.S. Department of Labor, we hold a job three to five years, with jobs held between ages 18 and 38 having the shortest duration. These days, the average length of a job is only six years. We may follow a particular occupational path, but we have become capitalist mercenaries of sorts, soldiers of fortune trying to survive a series of job changes. If government isn't doing a good job in working for us while we are working for it, we then fail to utilize the most constant of our life's relationships. Because of that, we need more than ever before to be a partner in that relationship. Unless we enhance the sense of daily choice in our lives, our lives become determined by events beyond our control, which weakens our moral choice.

Compound Capitalism does not forget the importance of retirement as a time in life for needed security. It more tangibly re-enforces the idea of even greater financial opportunity starting at birth, producing all the while by intent, and greatly expanding the benefits for retirement years. This solution is, at once, both a financial plan and a philosophy for a happier pursuit of happiness. Maybe you want to play in a jazz band or do embroidery? As a collateral benefit, we believe also that these differences in self-esteem and outlook gained through rewarded productivity, promotes the freedom to change one's normal vocation at an earlier age, if so desired, devoting more of one's time and ability to a preferred occupation or avocation, or at least of having that option.

AARP has joined the chorus for reasoned change. This is the best good-citizen-chance for the nearly 40 million members of AARP to speak out, as not one among them would lose one cent of promised benefits by this proposal, and therefore, will never have to look a child or grandchild in the eye evasively, burdened by the guilt or shame of profiting at their expense. Even better is that this opportunity will be what saves future recipients from reductions in expected benefits.

We wish to build upon the greater numbers of those who may be considered naturally able, but otherwise asset-capital deprived. In this broader sense, capitalizing future productivity now also helps those later proven deprived in some other regard, like illness or accident, better positioning a nation to assist those for whom luck-of-the-draw has permanently or temporarily run out.

That philosophy does not intend to create any condition for the redistribution of wealth or income by government fiat, but only to capitalize productive assets available at birth to accomplish instead the opportunity for wealth by productive design and with inheritable property being only one of many compounded catalysts in that design. In the sense of further sharing with those unable to help themselves, we embrace both compassion and assistance, since all citizens are included. Let's call that *'productive philanthropy.'*

And even those in need, having also been enrolled at birth, benefit—perhaps the most. That is because everyone's potential has been capitalized, including those for whom fate has precluded its future realization. Finally, we are not promoting the institution of retirement as our energizing notion, but the idea of more productive living for a lifetime. Retirement is merely an arbitrary phase in that greater continuum. We believe this combines both a useful and practical platform.

Our *'get out of jail free'* debt escape hatch is closer than you might imagine. In fact, it's been there for some time. The first step toward it is your recognition of the fact that you are a participating shareholder of a democratic capitalist market enterprise. Both institutions and words can have differing interpretations, depending upon both the context and their placement in our minds. Often, by reversing a more common pattern of thought, we gain new and useful insights just from changing our point of view.

What if it were legal to change your lucky number after-the-fact, both for yourself and for nearly a million dollars

in retirement security for America's unborn citizens? And what if every new citizen could do it too—every single one?

It is legal—and we can. This is an opportunity to reevaluate our potential for future well-being, health and education, and to tell ourselves whether or not we would rather participate in a more cooperative world.

What are we waiting for? You learned how to change your number. You were surprised at how easy it was, and even more, you have discovered how changing the numbers for one multiplies all the winners. That is *Compound Capitalism.*

In order to compound the numbers of shareholders, we must begin by compounding money. In order to begin compounding money, we must have it. In order to have it, we must save it and spur the growth of enterprise when the opportunity is presented.

All of those conditions are present now.

We have recognized that 'capital' is the result of releasing the asset-value energy contained in something else. We have recognized that the 'something else' can generate surplus assets from its own value. This all springs from a prior belief that assets must be fixed and realized in a particular subject. The value of future taxes and good citizenship are real values contained in something else. That something else is *'Us.'* That is measurable, at least on average. We are trying to generate surplus assets from that value. Perhaps it is just good fortune that the U.S. now has the chance to become *'Us'*?

As a justification for establishing property rights in future productivity, if a person does not own his/her future productivity, who owns it? But since it is inherent in and inseparable from its source of energizing productive power, it is already private property with value to its owner. The real question is, *"How much is it worth?"* Our study does not take us far enough to answer how man's reserves of greater potential are properly valued. We think, however, we know how they might be tapped, and that we are looking in the right place.

We have tried to look far beyond the untapped value hidden in human capital, a value we believe can be brought to life as if by magic by the vision of what might be. That process of looking beyond has, for us, identified what we believe to be is the missing link in capitalism; that once established, it will mature in direct relation to the evidence that can nurture further creative vision.

You'll note that a dollar bill and a hundred-dollar bill are the same paper, the same size—only the printing is different. It is not capital, but it is a representation of a certain established value. Assets need a formal value system to acknowledge their existence and worth. It is this recognition that allows it to be converted. Value, like energy, is a concept recognized by its effect more than its obvious substance.

If *Compound Capitalism* is to become a shareholding interest for all Americans, leaders and voting citizens must recognize it as a powerful source of energy, a renewable source, and insist upon it. In this sense both you and your government has a chance to vote for your future. You might look on this as a lesson plan prepared by other citizens who wish you well.

Why do governments build highways, airports, ports, dams, hydroelectric facilities, fund education, medicine, research—all the things we would not live so well without? Why do democratic republics go to the trouble of trying to elect the best persons to office if we don't also hope that they will contribute to making the profit-making ability of our enterprises and our citizens vastly better?

People have been thinking and writing about capitalism for over 250 years. It is possible that a capitalism that is more inclusive is more productive, because it involves more available minds to make contributions—to be both engaged and excited. This is a time when a revival of capitalism is in order, not the ownership of land, resources and/or property controlled more and more by government, but in expanding the ownership reach of we citizen owners.

Perhaps a single individual's mental efforts sometimes provide significant answers, but there is little doubt that too few of us ask others enough questions. That's why it is important that we see ourselves as shareholders, because the compounding of ideas between people engaged in asking important questions together is a much more powerful route to answers.

We can solve the problem of increasing the potential of all age groups by allowing the opportunity for personal accomplishment to flourish. Unbelievably, it is that simple. We want to take an incentive for success that is built into every human model and put it to work—tomorrow.

Compound Capitalism is not only powerful enough to make accomplishment self-fulfilling, but it is a property right within each of us. Using it may not make each life a stunning masterpiece, but as individual works of art, life's brushstrokes will be much improved. The way other people see us does influence the way we see ourselves. That is true, because each of us, knowing our story has a happy ending, will give much more pleasure in the telling.

There are many good social purposes, only some of which merit universal support. We firmly believe a great nation can and should sustain a system that provides bedrock retirement income, healthcare and educational security upon which further attainment can be built.

This is an acknowledgement of shareholder citizenship long overdue, only different in structural design and productive purpose. However, its support argument does not entail required agreement that obligations occurring far into the future are best handled by using current income for fulfillment. **We have used compound interest and interests and put them together.**

The public does have money for social purposes, but not unlimited money for everyone's special need or envy fulfillment. Our position accepts that there are trade-offs in life when one good is often chosen in lieu of another—or when fate deals each of us differing hands. There is no full-service cornucopia of *'make a wish'* granting, so every *'compound capital'* penny counts toward increasing productivity, responsibility, but not welfare.

This line of thinking does not favor any special interest group, political party, any particular category of individual or any type of corporation or business, but is of value to all, as every individual gets 'just' treatment, hardly possible under any other definition of democracy, constitutional or otherwise. This is truly an example of equality into which every future American citizen can be

born, if we demand it. Furthermore, the self-interest of bi-partisan politics cannot help but admire a system that produces personal and national wealth in the bargain with equal treatment under the law.

Should we have concerns using ethical and moral terms as components in the ranking of economic values? Is there a reason for both economic and social justice to be presented only in ways that will eliminate the chances of civil disobedience? We think not.

The essence of democratic freedom contains responsibility for the value judgments of our institutions, our fellow citizens and our personal behavior. In return, we expect that our personal pursuits of happiness include the understanding that the well-being and capabilities of other citizens are to be encouraged and facilitated, all our nation's potentials magnified—that we are cooperative beings.

As good citizens we cannot have freedom without the constant obligation to judge how things are; what are our responsibilities to exercise the human potential? Moral order and sovereign power should be complimentary, not in opposition.

We need to be uncharacteristically moral when making decisions whose effects are realized among generations, and even more when the impact is over many generations, either felt as good vibrations or as high magnitude aftershocks. Although governments must make decisions that effect generations unborn, they should be made with the utmost of care—and we should let our voices be heard.

Our goal is not to satisfy any narrow vision of economic justice, but to set the stage for the advancement of more widespread meritorious well-being, not forcing it through redistribution without merit. A fair share does not mean taking what someone else has to even up the piles, but to create a pile of one's own from already existing assets.

As another unintended, but predictable consequence, our hope is that the alchemy of this model will prove useful to other nations trying to solve retirement security problems of their own, and at the same time, to increase the sizes of their respective pies. In fact, pies tend to multiply faster when more people have a taste of them. One must also realize that it isn't even just one pie, as different pies are continuously being created and shared in various ways throughout the world.

How many of us have remarked about how quickly a child becomes a teenager? We all have. The simple key we want you to remember is that from birth to 18 years is such a short time. After 18, that person may well pay payroll taxes, just like you. But it is a crucial time when you are talking about compound interest and the *'starting money'* has already tripled from $12,000 to $36,000. It is the economic equivalent to the educational Head-Start program. But it is so much more!

New Congressional Wisdom

Is there any better opportunity for government to satisfy long-term obligations with dollars discounted by over ninety-eight percent? Is there any citizen who wouldn't prefer to pay for life's biggest expenditures with such greatly discounted dollars?

Why Veto Victory?

Whatever faction our elected co-shareholders favor, all will be expected to hold mutual bedrock assumptions. Among these will be support for the rapid compounding of democratic capitalism—more is better. Perhaps you have not thought about the fact that up till now government has not had the opportunity to take advantage of true compound interest in its financial form. That is because, for the most part, government investments are for the shorter run; government does not just set aside money to earn interest. The reason is that there is never what one would call—spare money. Government needs the chance to earn $77 on a $1 investment. Now they will!

Henceforth, why should our inherited endowment be the battle to control our resources, to prevent their unreasonable confiscation by people insisting on selling us products or services we don't want to buy? If we could impart a reasoned solution, the struggle for available resources wouldn't have to be fought out in a battle of Darwinian survival between citizens and their government. Shame can serve society well, but it must be utilized.

We grant our government a monopoly over the use of force, both globally and domestically. Such uses may or may not be deemed moral, depending upon the circumstances and rules-of-the-game. That said, why wouldn't we grant the same leadership rights in an economic situation where success can be achieved without force—where moral considerations are already answered affirmatively.

Imagine that the House and Senate reached an impasse on how to provide retirement security for future generations.

That dilemma is not difficult, because no matter how they try, it has been difficult for them to think that far into the future, all the while not knowing what might change.

An imagined future Speaker of the House, one who had become famous for the quote, *"What if they all live to be a hundred?"* now said, *"Let's observe a period of silence. Let's gather our thoughts"*

And so they did, because they had tried everything else. Lo and behold, it worked, because one of the newly elected members rose slowly, cleared her throat, and said:

"Mr. President, members of the House and Senate. Last night, I was dreaming. There's a place where we can get the money we need, and for free. Better yet, it is a well that won't run dry. The vision in my dream asked me how we could offer free or government-enforced health care to uncovered millions that costs hundreds of billions and not accept retirement income and healthcare security that costs nothing? I couldn't answer. The vision then asked me how we could more than double food stamp costs and cover 44 million people and not cover 4 million new citizens with cost-free retirement? I was reminded that there is great merit in being clever at conflict resolution, but what's even better is to elevate facts over tactics. I was told: 'You must place reason as a first, not a last resort. Interest, compound interest!' That's what came to me while I dreamt.

"Hooray!" reverberated through the chamber walls.

Economist Paul Romer is now well connected with the concept of *'non-rival goods,'* an idea you'll remember that he also calls *'recipes,'* because as a cooking analogy they can be used by any number of people at the same time without wearing out the usefulness of the recipe. *Compound Capitalism* is just such a recipe, but one that governments don't often get the chance to use. But when they do, they must, because there isn't a better recipe, at least for now. It seems somehow appropriate that this recipe is in a 'cookbook.' Thank you for compounding your performance and personal interests in becoming a shareholder.

Based on 2015 U.S. payroll taxes of approximately $1 trillion dollars, elimination of the payroll tax would save $1 trillion dollars per year in 67 years, perhaps much sooner. (Of course, that's counting no increase in inflation or no increase in population by 2083, both of which are incorrect.) Today U.S. population is 324,180,737 and world population is 7,342,821,852. In 67 years--2083, world population is estimated at 10 billion and U.S. population at 432 million, a U.S. increase of slightly over 100 million persons. (Approximately a 30% + increase) Based on that, payroll taxes would be at least $1.25 trillion in 2083—67 years hence. Thus, U.S. savings of payroll tax then would be at least $1.25 trillions annually thereafter. That's 1,250 billions of dollars every year to increase wages, economic growth and tax revenues. The cost of *Compound Capitalism* is $60 billion annually, or 60 divided into 1,250 or 1/20th of that cost, which also adds **LES**, Lifetime Educational Support. You economists fool with the figures yourselves, but it seems more than a good bargain to us who count on our fingers.

Also saved each year after debt elimination is the interest on the national debt, so let's call that at least $500-600 billion dollars yearly assuming the debt grows not a cent larger. Then remember that the returns to **RSA** funds and **RHS** funds due to premature deaths of account holders averages at least $50-60 billion dollars per each year's new 4,000,000 enrollees after 67 years and annually thereafter. Then remember that the government enterprise also retains 4% of total **RSA** funds, which in 67 years is 4% of total compounded birth-year individual assets. ($615,000 times 4,000,000 at 4%, or $246 billion annually .) So assume that we find no *Big Bills Left on the Sidewalk,* not a cent, rather than the $2-3 trillion annual dollars suggested and clearly identified in the book, and you will still immediately recognize shareholding *Compound Capitalism* as a huge benefit for all. We must insist on skin-in-the-game as our evolutionary *Compound Capitalism.* Albert Einstein had it right!

Aristotle had a remarkable insight over 2,300 years ago, that what you can do with ideas increases by leaps and bounds when the thinking is focused on hidden potential rather than on that which is obvious.

The growth potential of man is the greatest of ideas—

AND IDEAS COMPOUND!

Appendix 1. Account Holder's Vested Value and Mortality Table

Based on Social Security "1999 - Period Life Table"
Assumption - 4 Million Births Per Year

Year	Cumulative Account Value	Account Holder Owner-ship	Expected Number of Deaths	Gov't Vesting Percent	Cumulative Account Value Transferred to Government
1	$8,536	0.00	28,160	1.00	$240,373,760
2	9,107	0.00	2,045	1.00	18,623,815
3	9,717	0.00	1,389	1.00	13,496,913
4	10,368	0.00	1,071	1.00	11,104,128
5	11,063	0.00	833	1.00	9,215,479
6	11,803	0.00	773	1.00	9,123,719
7	12,594	0.00	734	1.00	9,243,996
8	13,437	0.00	694	1.00	9,325,278
9	14,337	0.00	634	1.00	9,089,658
10	15,297	0.00	595	1.00	9,101,715
11	16,322	0.00	495	1.00	8,079,390
12	17,415	0.00	515	1.00	8,968,725
13	18,581	0.00	673	1.00	12,505,013
14	19,826	0.00	990	1.00	19,627,740
15	21,154	0.00	1,425	1.00	30,144,450
16	22,570	0.00	1,959	1.00	44,214,630
17	24,082	0.00	2,393	1.00	57,628,226
18	25,695	0.00	2,806	1.00	72,100,170
19	27,416	0.00	3,041	1.00	83,372,056
20	29,252	0.49	3,235	0.51	48,261,412

21	31,211	0.50	3,389	0.50	52,887,040
22	33,301	0.51	3,563	0.49	58,139,217
23	35,531	0.52	3,637	0.48	62,028,599
24	37,911	0.53	3,692	0.47	65,784,684
25	40,450	0.54	3,688	0.46	68,622,616
26	43,159	0.55	3,645	0.45	70,791,550
27	46,049	0.56	3,622	0.44	73,387,370
28	49,133	0.57	3,677	0.43	77,684,678
29	52,423	0.58	3,731	0.42	82,147,889
30	55,934	0.59	3,903	0.41	89,507,265
31	59,680	0.60	4,036	0.40	96,347,392
32	63,667	0.61	4,245	0.39	105,420,457
33	67,942	0.62	4,435	0.38	114,502,653
34	72,492	0.63	4,683	0.37	125,607,613
35	77,347	0.64	4,968	0.36	138,333,563
36	82,527	0.65	5,311	0.35	153,405,314
37	88,054	0.66	5,671	0.34	169,780,440
38	93,951	0.67	6,049	0.33	187,542,168
39	100,243	0.68	6,464	0.32	307,530,641
40	106,957	0.69	6,915	0.31	229,278,373
41	114,120	0.70	7,421	0.30	254,065,356
42	121,763	0.71	7,981	0.29	281,819,246
43	129,917	0.72	8,576	0.28	311,967,094

44	138,618	0.73	9,242	0.27	345,899,040
45	147,902	0.74	9,999	0.26	384,506,745
46	157,807	0.75	10,825	0.25	427,065,194
47	168,376	0.76	11,719	0.24	473,567,603
48	179,652	0.77	12,586	0.23	520,053,017
49	191,684	0.78	13,466	0.22	567,024,274
50	204,521	0.79	14,352	0.21	616,409,932
51	218,218	0.80	15,304	0.20	667,291,654
52	232,833	0.81	16,410	0.19	725,950,011
53	248,426	0.82	17,688	0.18	790,054,302
54	365,064	0.83	19,146	0.17	862,735,608
55	282,815	0.84	20,764	0.16	939,579,306
56	301,756	0.85	22,590	0.15	1,022,500,206
57	321,965	0.86	24,489	0.14	1,103,844,124
58	343,528	0.87	26,438	0.13	1,180,685,124
59	366,534	0.88	28,307	0.12	1,245,057,353
60	391,082	0.89	30,218	0.11	1,299,948,746
61	417,273	0.90	32,181	0.10	1,342,826,241
62	445,219	0.91	34,399	0.09	1,378,357,954
63	475,036	0.92	36,941	0.08	1,403,864,390
64	506,850	0.93	39,869	0.07	1,414,532,186
65	540,795	0.94	43,006	0.06	1,395,445,786
66	577,013	0.95	46,310	0.05	1,366,073,602
67	615,656	0.96	49,515	0.04	1,219,368,274
	TOTAL				$26,463,272,160

Appendix 2. Compound Interest Table

Account Holder's Invested Value				
Effects of Compounding Interest on Initial Investment of $8,000				
	Interest Rate			
Year	6.30%	6.50%	6.80%	7.30%
10	$15,885	$16,234	$16,771	$17,707
20	29,777	31,043	33,041	36,662
30	55,818	59,359	65,094	75,908
40	104,632	113,506	128,242	157,167
50	196,134	217,043	252,648	325,413
60	367,657	415,027	497,740	673,767
67	538,830	615,657	751,884	1,049,034

As you see, the magic of money doubling itself every few years produces astonishing results! So long as the account system is restricted so that account holders cannot dissipate the capital, the magic is preserved to the degree intended.

Appendix 3. Duplication of Effort: Ever Wonder Why California is Broke?

The Executive Order

Executive Order 13563 relates to "Improving Regulation and Regulatory Review." The Order reflects the view that:

"Our regulatory system must protect public health, welfare, safety, and our environment while promoting economic growth, innovation, competitiveness, and job creation. It must be based on the best available science. It must allow for public participation and an open exchange of ideas. It must promote predictability and reduce uncertainty. It must identify and use the best, most innovative, and least burdensome tools for achieving regulatory ends. It must take into account benefits and costs, both quantitative and qualitative. It must ensure that regulations are accessible, consistent, written in plain language, and easy to understand. It must measure, and seek to improve, the actual results of regulatory requirements"

In order to find savings in the way we manage the day-by-day institution of America, the enterprise, we not only have to look at the whole but some of the parts. **We call the parts States.** When we analyze States in order to see if they are places where we can save money by not duplicating efforts or services, or analyze America the (Federal) enterprise, we ask similar questions to both.

The first is: Is there more than one agency or regulator that concerns itself with a particular need or issue? Are we duplicating effort needlessly and wasting time and money? How can we save by consolidating responsibilities? We put the California's 11 packed pages of agencies here in the Appendix so as not to distress you overly, unless you wanted to take a peek voluntarily.

Of course, we already know that more general duplication of effort is rampant. This is neither a good way to provide adequate employment opportunity nor a frugal use of taxpayer dollars. We have used our most populous State to suggest that there are Big Bills opportunities surrounding us from which we can derive more billions in savings toward reducing both State and Federal debt levels, just by paying attention.

These are all California State Agencies

California Academic Performance Index (API) * California Access for Infants and Mothers * California Acupuncture Board * California Administrative Office of the Courts * California Adoptions Branch * California African American Museum * California Agricultural Export Program * California Agricultural Labor Relations Board * California Agricultural Statistics Service * California Air Resources Board (CARB) * California Allocation Board * California Alternative Energy and Advanced Transportation Financing Authority * California Animal Health and Food Safety Services * California Anti-Terrorism Information Center * California Apprenticeship Council * California Arbitration Certification Program * California Architects Board * California Area VI Developmental Disabilities Board * California Arts Council * California Asian Pacific Islander Legislative Caucus * California Assembly Democratic Caucus * California Assembly Republican Caucus * California Athletic Commission * California Attorney General * California Bay Conservation and Development Commission * California Bay-Delta Authority * California Bay-Delta Office * California Biodiversity Council * California Board for Geologists and

Geophysicists * California Board for Professional
Engineers and Land Surveyors * California Board of
Accountancy * California Board of Barbering and
Cosmetology * California Board of Behavioral Sciences *
California Board of Chiropractic Examiners * California
Board of Equalization (BOE) * California Board of Forestry
and Fire Protection * California Board of Guide Dogs for
the Blind * California Board of Occupational Therapy *
California Board of Optometry * California Board of
Pharmacy * California Board of Podiatric Medicine *
California Board of Prison Terms * California Board of
Psychology * California Board of Registered Nursing *
California Board of Trustees * California Board of
Vocational Nursing and Psychiatric Technicians *
California Braille and Talking Book Library * California
Building Standards Commission * California Bureau for
Private Postsecondary and Vocational Education *
California Bureau of Automotive Repair * California
Bureau of Electronic and Appliance Repair * California
Bureau of Home Furnishings and Thermal Insulation *
California Bureau of Naturopathic Medicine * California
Bureau of Security and Investigative Services * California
Bureau of State Audits * California Business Agency *
California Business Investment Services (CalBIS) *
California Business Permit Information (CalGOLD) *
California Business Portal * California Business,
Transportation and Housing Agency * California Cal
Grants * California CalJOBS * California Cal-Learn
Program * California CalVet Home Loan Program *
California Career Resource Network * California Cemetery
and Funeral Bureau * California Center for Analytical
Chemistry * California Center for Distributed Learning *
California Center for Teaching Careers (Teach California) *
California Chancellors Office * California Charter Schools *
California Children and Families Commission * California
Children and Family Services Division * California

Citizens Compensation Commission * California Civil
Rights Bureau * California Coastal Commission *
California Coastal Conservancy * California Code of
Regulations * California Collaborative Projects with UC
Davis * California Commission for Jobs and Economic
Growth * California Commission on Aging * California
Commission on Health and Safety and Workers
Compensation * California Commission on Judicial
Performance * California Commission on State Mandates *
California Commission on Status of Women * California
Commission on Teacher Credentialing * California
Commission on the Status of Women * California
Committee on Dental Auxiliaries * California Community
Colleges Chancellors Office, Junior Colleges * California
Community Colleges Chancellors Office * California
Complaint Mediation Program * California Conservation
Corps * California Constitution Revision Commission *
California Consumer Hotline * California Consumer
Information Center * California Consumer Information *
California Consumer Services Division * California
Consumers and Families Agency * California Contractors
State License Board * California Corrections Standards
Authority * California Council for the Humanities *
California Council on Criminal Justice * California Council
on Developmental Disabilities * California Court Reporters
Board * California Courts of Appeal * California Crime and
Violence Prevention Center * California Criminal Justice
Statistics Center * California Criminalist Institute Forensic
Library * California CSGnet Network Management *
California Cultural and Historical Endowment * California
Cultural Resources Division * California Curriculum and
Instructional Leadership Branch * California Data
Exchange Center * California Data Management Division *
California Debt and Investment Advisory Commission *
California Delta Protection Commission * California
Democratic Caucus * California Demographic Research

Unit * California Dental Auxiliaries * California
Department of Aging * California Department of Alcohol
and Drug Programs * California Department of Alcoholic
Beverage Control Appeals Board * California Department
of Alcoholic Beverage Control * California Department of
Boating and Waterways (Cal Boating) * California
Department of Child Support Services (CDCSS) *
California Department of Community Services and
Development * California Department of Conservation *
California Department of Consumer Affairs * California
Department of Corporations * California Department of
Corrections and Rehabilitation * California Department of
Developmental Services * California Department of
Education * California Department of Fair Employment
and Housing * California Department of Finance *
California Department of Financial Institutions * California
Department of Fish and Game * California Department of
Food and Agriculture * California Department of Forestry
and Fire Protection (CDF) * California Department of
General Services * California Department of General
Services, Office of State Publishing * California
Department of Health Care Services * California
Department of Housing and Community Development *
California Department of Industrial Relations (DIR) *
California Department of Insurance * California
Department of Justice Firearms Division * California
Department of Justice Opinion Unit * California
Department of Justice, Consumer Information, Public
Inquiry Unit * California Department of Justice * California
Department of Managed Health Care * California
Department of Mental Health * California Department of
Motor Vehicles (DMV) * California Department of
Personnel Administration * California Department of
Pesticide Regulation * California Department of Public
Health * California Department of Real Estate * California
Department of Rehabilitation * California Department of

Social Services Adoptions Branch * California Department
of Social Services * California Department of Technology
Services Training Center (DTSTC) * California Department
of Technology Services (DTS) * California Department of
Toxic Substances Control * California Department of
Transportation (Caltrans) * California Department of
Veterans Affairs (CalVets) * California Department of
Water Resources * California Departmento de Vehiculos
Motorizados * California Digital Library * California
Disabled Veteran Business Enterprise Certification
Program * California Division of Apprenticeship Standards
* California Division of Codes and Standards * California
Division of Communicable Disease Control * California
Division of Engineering * California Division of
Environmental and Occupational Disease Control *
California Division of Gambling Control * California
Division of Housing Policy Development * California
Division of Labor Standards Enforcement * California
Division of Labor Statistics and Research * California
Division of Land and Right of Way * California Division of
Land Resource Protection * California Division of Law
Enforcement General Library * California Division of
Measurement Standards * California Division of Mines and
Geology * California Division of Occupational Safety and
Health (Cal/OSHA) * California Division of Oil, Gas and
Geothermal Resources * California Division of Planning
and Local Assistance * California Division of Recycling *
California Division of Safety of Dams * California Division
of the State Architect * California Division of Tourism *
California Division of Workers Compensation Medical
Unit * California Division of Workers Compensation *
California Economic Assistance, Business and Community
Resources * California Economic Strategy Panel *
California Education and Training Agency * California
Education Audit Appeals Panel * California Educational
Facilities Authority * California Elections Division *

California Electricity Oversight Board * California
Emergency Management Agency * California Emergency
Medical Services Authority * California Employment
Development Department (EDD) * California Employment
Information State Jobs * California Employment Training
Panel * California Energy Commission * California
Environment and Natural Resources Agency * California
Environmental Protection Agency (Cal/EPA) * California
Environmental Resources Evaluation System (CERES) *
California Executive Office * California Export Laboratory
Services * California Exposition and State Fair (Cal Expo) *
California Fair Political Practices Commission * California
Fairs and Expositions Division * California Film
Commission * California Fire and Resource Assessment
Program * California Firearms Division * California Fiscal
Services * California Fish and Game Commission *
California Fisheries Program Branch * California
Floodplain Management * California Foster Youth Help *
California Franchise Tax Board (FTB) * California Fraud
Division * California Gambling Control Commission *
California Geographic Information Systems Council (GIS) *
California Geological Survey * California Government
Claims and Victim Compensation Board * California
Governors Committee for Employment of Disabled
Persons * California Governors Mentoring Partnership *
California Governors Office of Emergency Services *
California Governors Office of Homeland Security *
California Governors Office of Planning and Research *
California Governors Office * California Grant and
Enterprise Zone Programs HCD Loan * California Health
and Human Services Agency * California Health and
Safety Agency * California Healthy Families Program *
California Hearing Aid Dispensers Bureau * California
High-Speed Rail Authority * California Highway Patrol
(CHP) * California History and Culture Agency *
California Horse Racing Board * California Housing

Finance Agency * California Indoor Air Quality Program *
California Industrial Development Financing Advisory
Commission * California Industrial Welfare Commission *
California InFoPeople * California Information Center for
the Environment * California Infrastructure and Economic
Development Bank (I-Bank) * California Inspection
Services * California Institute for County Government *
California Institute for Education Reform * California
Integrated Waste Management Board * California
Interagency Ecological Program * California Job Service *
California Junta Estatal de Personal * California Labor and
Employment Agency * California Labor and Workforce
Development Agency * California Labor Market
Information Division * California Land Use Planning
Information Network (LUPIN) * California Lands
Commission * California Landscape Architects Technical
Committee * California Latino Legislative Caucus *
California Law Enforcement Branch * California Law
Enforcement General Library * California Law Revision
Commission * California Legislative Analyst's Office *
California Legislative Black Caucus * California Legislative
Counsel * California Legislative Division * California
Legislative Information * California Legislative Lesbian,
Gay, Bisexual, and Transgender (LGBT) Caucus *
California Legislature Internet Caucus * California Library
Development Services * California License and Revenue
Branch * California Major Risk Medical Insurance Program
* California Managed Risk Medical Insurance Board *
California Maritime Academy * California Marketing
Services * California Measurement Standards * California
Medical Assistance Commission * California Medical Care
Services * California Military Department * California
Mining and Geology Board * California Museum for
History, Women, and the Arts * California Museum
Resource Center * California National Guard * California
Native American Heritage Commission * California

Natural Community Conservation Planning Program *
California New Motor Vehicle Board * California Nursing
Home Administrator Program * California Occupational
Safety and Health Appeals Board * California
Occupational Safety and Health Standards Board *
California Ocean Resources Management Program *
California Office of Administrative Hearings * California
Office of Administrative Law * California Office of AIDS *
California Office of Bi-national Border Health * California
Office of Child Abuse Prevention * California Office of
Deaf Access * California Office of Emergency Services
(OES) * California Office of Environmental Health Hazard
Assessment * California Office of Fiscal Services *
California Office of Fleet Administration * California Office
of Health Insurance Portability and Accountability Act
(HIPAA) Implementation (CalOHI) * California Office of
Historic Preservation * California Office of Homeland
Security * California Office of Human Resources *
California Office of Legal Services * California Office of
Legislation * California Office of Lieutenant Governor *
California Office of Military and Aerospace Support *
California Office of Mine Reclamation * California Office of
Natural Resource Education * California Office of Privacy
Protection * California Office of Public School Construction
* California Office of Real Estate Appraisers * California
Office of Risk and Insurance Management * California
Office of Services to the Blind * California Office of Spill
Prevention and Response * California Office of State
Publishing (OSP) * California Office of Statewide Health
Planning and Development * California Office of Systems
Integration * California Office of the Inspector General *
California Office of the Ombudsman * California Office of
the Patient Advocate * California Office of the President *
California Office of the Secretary for Education * California
Office of the State Fire Marshal * California Office of the
State Public Defender * California Office of Traffic Safety *

California Office of Vital Records * California Online
Directory * California Operations Control Office *
California Opinion Unit * California Outreach and
Technical Assistance Network (OTAN) * California Park
and Recreation Commission * California Peace Officer
Standards and Training (POST) * California Performance
Review (CPR) * California Permit Information for Business
(CalGOLD) * California Physical Therapy Board *
California Physician Assistant Committee * California
Plant Health and Pest Prevention Services * California
Policy and Evaluation Division * California Political
Reform Division * California Pollution Control Financing
Authority * California Polytechnic State University, San
Luis Obispo * California Postsecondary Education
Commission * California Prevention Services * California
Primary Care and Family Health * California Prison
Industry Authority * California Procurement Division *
California Public Employees Retirement System (CalPERS)
* California Public Employment Relations Board (PERB) *
California Public Utilities Commission (PUC) * California
Real Estate Services Division * California Refugee
Programs Branch * California Regional Water Quality
Control Boards * California Registered Veterinary
Technician Committee * California Registrar of Charitable
Trusts * California Republican Caucus * California
Research and Development Division * California Research
Bureau * California Resources Agency * California
Respiratory Care Board * California Rivers Assessment *
California Rural Health Policy Council * California Safe
Schools * California San Francisco Bay Conservation and
Development Commission * California San Gabriel and
Lower Los Angeles Rivers and Mountains Conservancy *
California San Joaquin River Conservancy * California
School to Career * California Science Center * California
Scripps Institution of Oceanography * California Secretary
of State Business Portal * California Secretary of State *

California Seismic Safety Commission * California Self
Insurance Plans (SIP) * California Senate Office of Research
* California Small Business and Disabled Veteran Business
Enterprise Certification Program * California Small
Business Development Center Program * California Smart
Growth Caucus * California Smog Check Information
Center * California Spatial Information Library * California
Special Education Division * California Speech-Language
Pathology and Audiology Board * California Standardized
Testing and Reporting (STAR) * California Standards and
Assessment Division * California State Administrative
Manual (SAM) * California State Allocation Board *
California State and Consumer Services Agency *
California State Architect * California State Archives *
California State Assembly * California State Association of
Counties (CSAC) * California State Board of Education *
California State Board of Food and Agriculture *California
Office of the Chief Information Officer (OCIO) * California
State Children's Trust Fund * California State
Compensation Insurance Fund * California State Contracts
Register Program * California State Contracts Register *
California State Controller * California State Council on
Developmental Disabilities (SCDD) * California State
Disability Insurance (SDI) * California State Fair (Cal Expo)
* California State Jobs Employment Information *
California State Lands Commission * California State
Legislative Portal * California State Legislature * California
State Library Catalog * California State Library Services
Bureau * California State Library * California State Lottery
* California State Mediation and Conciliation Service *
California State Mining and Geology Board * California
State Park and Recreation Commission * California State
Parks * California State Personnel Board * California State
Polytechnic University, Pomona * California State Railroad
Museum * California State Science Fair * California State
Senate * California State Summer School for Mathematics

and Science (COSMOS) * California State Summer School for the Arts * California State Superintendent of Public Instruction * California State Teachers Retirement System (CalSTRS) * California State Treasurer * California State University Center for Distributed Learning * California State University, Bakersfield * California State University, Channel Islands * California State University, Chico * California State University, Dominguez Hills * California State University, East Bay * California State University, Fresno * California State University, Fullerton * California State University, Long Beach * California State University, Los Angeles * California State University, Monterey Bay * California State University, Northridge * California State University, Sacramento * California State University, San Bernardino * California State University, San Marcos * California State University, Stanislaus * California State University (CSU) * California State Water Project Analysis Office * California State Water Project * California State Water Resources Control Board * California Structural Pest Control Board * California Student Aid Commission * California Superintendent of Public Instruction * California Superior Courts * California Tahoe Conservancy * California Task Force on Culturally and Linguistically Competent Physicians and Dentists * California Tax Information Center * California Technology and Administration Branch Finance * California Telecommunications Division * California Telephone Medical Advice Services (TAMS) * California Transportation Commission * California Travel and Transportation Agency * California Unclaimed Property Program * California Unemployment Insurance Appeals Board * California Unemployment Insurance Program * California Uniform Construction Cost Accounting Commission * California Veterans Board * California Veterans Memorial * California Veterinary Medical Board and Registered Veterinary Technician Examining

Committee * California Veterinary Medical Board *
California Victim Compensation and Government Claims
Board * California Volunteers * California Voter
Registration * California Water Commission * California
Water Environment Association (COWPEA) * California
Water Resources Control Board * California Welfare to
Work Division * California Wetlands Information System *
California Wildlife and Habitat Data Analysis Branch *
California Wildlife Conservation Board * California
Wildlife Programs Branch * California Work Opportunity
and Responsibility to Kids (CalWORKs) * California
Workers Compensation Appeals Board * California
Workforce and Labor Development Agency * California
Workforce Investment Board * California Youth Authority
(CYA) * Central Valley Flood Protection Board * Center for
California Studies * Colorado River Board of California *
Counting California * Dental Board of California * Health
Insurance Plan of California (PacAdvantage) * Humboldt
State University * Jobs with the State of California *
Judicial Council of California * Learn California * Library
of California * Lieutenant Governors Commission for One
California * Little Hoover Commission (on California State
Government Organization and Economy) * Medical Board
of California * Medi-Cal * Osteopathic Medical Board of
California * Physical Therapy Board of California * Regents
of the University of California * San Diego State University
* San Francisco State University * San Jose State University
* Santa Monica Mountains Conservancy * State Bar of
California * Supreme Court of California * Teach California
* University of California * University of California,
Berkeley * University of California, Davis * University of
California, Hastings College of the Law * University of
California, Irvine * University of California, Los Angeles *
University of California, Merced * University of California,
Riverside * University of California, San Diego * University
of California, San Francisco * University of California,

Santa Barbara * University of California, Santa Cruz *
Veterans Home of California

Appendix 4. A Short Social Security Entitlement History

To remind you of how much better Compound Capitalism is, let's review some Social Security history, why it has served its time and why we are now seeking release.

Great banks and great governments develop financial policies and products that their customers can use. In developing the current Social Security system, government created a 'junk bond,' an instrument of dubious value.

In fact, if this product were available for use or sale in a competitive financial market today, nobody would buy it, not one person. Not only would there by no buyers, but no one in their rational mind would offer the current system as a product; unless the buyer was forced to buy it and the seller didn't have the threat of punishment to intimidate any who would refuse. Ask any financial advisor to determine if the present system has sufficient merit; whether or not its product would be purchased on a voluntary basis when neither the future cost nor benefits can be guaranteed nor when your premature death or being of the wrong race or gender can produce unfair benefits?

"Four score and seven years ago ..." Think back to the tragedy of the American Civil War in which we killed the future citizen opportunities of our own people in huge numbers, 620,000 Americans lost their lives, over 200 times 9/11. We had few black citizens then—no women citizens.

States rights prevailed over a latent but missing sense of mutual belonging. That came close to defeating the Constitutional *'self-evident'* opportunities for black and white, male and female, urban or agricultural, no matter one's religion. We should have learned the perils of segregation then, that skin-in-the-game shareholding is much better than sharecropping. It's never too late to learn, but it can also become too late to put even good lessons to use. Sometimes there is no preceding lesson to teach us better.

In 1929, the dark, angry clouds of the 20th Century's Great Depression arrived in October as a full-blown tornado. It was still at destructive gale force in 1935. The realization came quickly that this was not the usual business recession and the storm lasted beyond a decade.

As unemployment reached 25% and as the years dragged on, desperation became a daily emotion for all too many. For some, it seemed as though the collapse of capitalism predicted by the Marxists had become a self-fulfilling prophecy. (Although later known to have been a failure of monetary policy.)

At the time, however, conditions seemed ripe for revolt, a time to paint a providential new picture of a secure old age for America's disenchanted millions. And to do this with non-existent money seemed just as natural—after all, the day of reckoning was somewhere in the future—but the time of need was now. More important was to promote the idea that there would be a future worth having.

Now, financially threatened social insurance systems worldwide are forced to find structural solutions to achieve similar purposes. What was once a safety net has become a snare, and with little surprise, since the financing method, where current workers pay for current retirees, defies all market logic. Not surprisingly however, attempts at the same scheme in the public sector would today be deemed criminal acts, correctly referred to as either Ponzi or pyramid schemes. Sooner rather than later, most such frauds run into the truth of simple mathematics. That is because the money is never put to productive use beyond paying off prior investors. The scheme works only so long as an endless supply of new victims can be found, but when they decline in number, for whatever reason, the whole financial structure collapses. Noted showman P.T. Barnum was right in saying: *"A sucker is born every minute."* Even he was not anticipating needing millions of them.

Ponzi schemes and pyramids? Let's take a look back at another famous pyramid.

Built by the pharaoh Khufu in 2560 BC, Egypt's Great Pyramid of Giza, the greatest of the pyramids, has eroded by only 30 of its 481 feet, and in 4567 years, only six-tenths of one percent! The architectural margin for error of any side was less than one tenth of one percent and for 43 centuries it was the tallest structure in the world. It is the only survivor of the Seven Ancient Wonders.

One rising to the top of Giza's Great Pyramid today can look back over forty-five centuries of history. Yet, after barely more than a half-century, a visitor to the Social Security pyramid, even from atop Washington's Monument, can look back only upon shambles. Structures not built for survival cannot be saved. They must be built anew and of better stone.

Egypt's Great Pyramid was built to support a royal journey into the afterlife. America's Social Security pyramid was also built to support a journey into the afterlife, the afterlife of work. It is a structure eroding rapidly and radically changing in shape. What happened? America's social pyramid, erected in 1935, paid its first check in 1940, but could not stand the pressures and changes of time; time not measured by centuries or millenniums. But in the shortest passage of time, troubles were foreseen—broad cracks in the foundation. Like physical architecture, social architecture not well designed is soon bound for the wrecking ball; not worthy of being saved because even its basic outlines are no longer recognizable, even to the keenest of observers. Whereas it took twenty years to build Egypt's wonder of the world, after only the first twenty years of payments, the world began to wonder about the crumbling American pyramid.

The first mistake was in expectations beyond promised intentions. F.D.R. said, while signing the law:

"We can never insure 100% of the population against 100% of the hazards and vicissitudes of life, but we have tried to frame a law which will give some measure of protection to the average citizen and to his family ... against poverty-ridden old age."

Franklin Roosevelt's political successors would have done well to remember 'this measure of protection' and most certainly have not. They have forgotten or ignored what he said.

When the first monthly checks were issued in 1940, America was still in the throes of depression and the pyramid of retirement consumption seemed built of solid gold, its reflected gleam so bright that it blinded a dejected nation's reason—but not the political eye or its appetite. It also had a very broad base at the bottom, **forty-two persons paying in for every one drawing out. Now there are 2 paying in for every one recipient.**

An account from 1982 gives an interesting timetable.

In January 1940, Ida Fuller of Brattleboro, Vt., who had paid a total of $22 in Social Security taxes, received Social Security check No. #1 for $22.54. Shortly after her 100th birthday, in December 1974, Fuller drew her last monthly check, for $112.60. By then she had collected $20,944.42 in return for her modest $22!

Characteristic of the preponderance of the earlier Social Security beneficiaries, Ida Fuller's large return seemed to make the investments appear far too good to be true. It even reinforced the idea that payroll taxes were invested, which they were not, promoting a fantasy that world-savvy politicians were loath to correct.

At the time of the first actual payment in 1940 the life expectancy wasn't even as long as the earliest possible age of retirement, age 62. **What we also know is that even though President Roosevelt made it unmistakably clear that it was not to be a retirement plan, but only a platform upon which building an individual savings would be a necessity, the actual result has proved that recipients viewed it otherwise.**

Fast-forward till today. Observe that for two-thirds of present retirees, it is their only retirement security. It was in recognizing this statistic that political decisions continued to raise both benefits and payroll deductions over the past 76 years.

Today, 7% of households have no financial assets and 91% of the total income of the lowest 20% of earners comes from government. What this also proves is that left to our own decisions, too many people have not taken responsible steps to assure their own well-being. What that suggests is that most of us would fare considerably better were there plans that delivered savings into our future somewhat automatically, like deductions at work or some other type of built-in savings, like an insurance policy that protects against making a big mistake.

Very simply, the basic security assumptions have been wrong. All wrong! There will soon be 2.3 worker payees for every retiree when there were 42 for each retiree at the system's inception. Because of better food and agriculture, better disease control and better medical advances, people live longer, healthier lives—much longer.

After over two dozen changes since inception, the system has failed in every regard by which any business enterprise might be evaluated, and by the virtue of being a government program, can continue to make promises only through a combination of raising taxes, creating debt from general revenue funds, cutting benefits, raising retirement ages or some combination of the preceding.

When Social Security was designed over seventy years ago, our understanding of certain financial principles was also in infancy. Since then we have learned a great deal about how markets work, how risk may be calculated and managed and about the inter-generational aspects of public retirement finance. In the interim, we have come from the Depression to become a nation of great wealth— the most affluent of the wealthy nations. In that process we have learned much about voluntary personal retirement vehicles. We have learned how to design better legal and regulatory structures, including dealing with the moral hazard of having individuals reach retirement age with no source of long-term income. It is desirable to relieve society from the challenge of one's own care and maintenance. We cannot be absolved of responsibility.

After 70+ years of Social Security trial and error—cutting and pasting—no one will say it hasn't been well tested or that the score is not final. There are no extra innings. The factual evidence, examined backwards and forward by economists, accountants and public intellectuals is that PAYGO, (Pay-as-you-go) retirement security systems cannot work in an era where life expectancy is on the rise and birth rates are low. That is a flawed Ponzi scheme more worthy of Bernie Madoff than elected legislators, except that under the ongoing legislative sponsors, far more people have been hoodwinked.

Take the revealing example of Nobel Laureate and distinguished economist Paul Samuelson as late as 1967:

"The beauty of social insurance is that it is actuarially unsound. Everyone who reaches retirement age is given benefit privileges that far exceed anything he has put in ... how is this possible? It stems from the fact that the national product is growing at compound interest ... Always there are more youths than old folks in a growing population ... A growing nation is the greatest Ponzi game ever contrived."

Dr. Samuelson had the Ponzi concept pegged right, but sadly, considering his lofty reputation, the predicted outcome was uncharacteristically wrong. So long as the workforce grew by around 1.5% a year with wages rising at around 2.5%, the system seemed to offer a decent rate-of-return, around 4% annually. How wrong can arguably smart people be? It turns out that what Dr. Samuelson said was not far off—at least when he said it.

However, the day of reckoning was not long in coming. Those born in 1934 were the last group to hope that their rate of return would equal that of Treasury Bills. For most people retiring in the future, the return would be greater had they buried the money in the backyard, as there will have been a negative return.

Quite a chagrined and chastened Paul Samuelson told a different story in 1985, a short 18 years after his initial and infamous Ponzi quote, writing:

"When population growth slows down, so that we no longer have the comfortable Ponzi rate of growth or we even begin to register a decline in total numbers, then the thorns along the primrose path reveal themselves with a vengeance."

Enough said, other than a word of thankful respect to Dr. Samuelson, who, unlike too many of those who might actually change directions, was strong enough to admit error. That is a mark of greatness.

Chain letters and chain checks require an increasing base number of people (pigeons) to come in at the bottom of the pyramid as a much smaller group exits (retirees) at the top. As long as the stabilizing base keeps broadening, the final day of reckoning is postponed and Mr. Ponzi stays out of trouble. (A temporary pardon, not a *'get out of jail free'* card.)

"I am going to talk about the fiscal unsustainability of all this in a moment. I am reminded of what my friend, Herb Stein, once said to us in the Nixon White House. "If something is unsustainable it tends to stop." Or, if you prefer the old adage, "If your horse dies, we suggest you dismount." I think the only issue is how we dismount what is clearly morally, socially, and increasingly fiscally unsustainable."

—Alan Greenspan, Past Chairman, The Federal Reserve

When we say Social Security is 'insolvent', it is not meant to convey the same meaning attached to the word 'indigent', as in a beggar on a street corner with a sign asking for a handout. This is a very rich and well-heeled beggar we are describing, one who owns a special printing press and the legal right to print his own money. That man with the press would be insolvent if he was an ordinary man without a printing press.

If our well-heeled beggar were running an ordinary business, for example, that business would be out of money. And in truth, even though America is a unique type of organization or enterprise, even it will soon to be out of interest free money, because even the newly printed bills must be accounted for; and once accounted for, every dollar will then be called 'borrowed' and interest will have to be paid on every dollar of debt. So it won't be free money, but the most expensive kind of money—debt.

In 2011, William Gale and Benjamin Harris of the Brookings Institution and the Tax Policy Center said this:

"Although the **unsustainable nature** of federal fiscal policy has been discussed at least since the 1980s, the problem has increased in importance and urgency in recent years for several reasons. First, the medium-term projections have deteriorated significantly. Second, the issues driving the long-term projections—in particular, the retirement of the baby boomers and the aging of the population and resulting pressure on Medicare and to some extent Social Security—which were several decades away in the 1980s, are now imminent. Third, questions about the rest of the world's appetite for U.S. government debt are growing louder, as the United States has changed from a net creditor country in 1980 to a vast net borrower currently. Fourth, many other countries around the world and many of the 50 American states currently face daunting fiscal prospects."

Without *Compound Capitalism*, the policy changes that are needed to close the fiscal gap represent enormous shifts relative to current policy. By way of comparison, in 2008, for example, the individual income tax raised about 6.4 percent of GDP in revenue.

Closing today's fiscal gap of 9 percent of GDP will be a Herculean task, requiring broad and deep adjustments to existing spending and tax programs, and quite likely new revenue sources as well.

In the future and if left as is, future obligations of Social Security, Medicare and Medicaid will fully devastate our nation's economy. Current economists, actuaries and accountants also like talking about future account balances using the term *'unsustainable'* instead of bankrupt.

We are on another disruptive path, but instead of being geographical, North vs. South, it has become economic, generational, and educational; indebtedness vs. wealth, old vs. young, and competitive vs. falling behind. Today's is not a conflict between geographical strangers in national disagreement, but with our own flesh and blood already unified as a single nation and family.

"It is rather for us to be here dedicated to the great task remaining before us ... a new birth of freedom."

—Abraham Lincoln

Bibliography

Bacevich, Andrew J.—The Limits of Power—Henry Holt & Company, 2008

Baker, Raymond W.—Capitalism's Achilles Heel—Wiley, 2005

Barrett, Scott—Why Cooperate?—Oxford, 2007

Baumol, William J., Litan, Robert E., Schramm, Carl J.— Good Capitalism, Bad Capitalism—Yale University Press, 2007

Baumol, William J.—The Microtheoory of Innovative Entrepreneurship—Princeton University Press, 2010

Becker, Gary S.—Human Capital—University of Chicago Press. 3rd Edition, 1993

Becker, Gary S. and Becker, Guity Nashat—The Economics of Life—McGraw Hill, 1997

Berlin, Isaiah—The Sense of Reality—Edited by Henry Hardy—Farrar, Straus and Giroux, 1996

Berlin, Isaiah—The Power of Ideas—Edited by Henry Hardy—Princeton University Press, 2002
 Paperback Edition

Bobbitt, Philip—Terror and Consent—Knopf, 2008

Borden, Karl J. and Rounds, Charles E., Jr.,—Cato Project on Social Security Privatization.

Social Security Paper #25. A Proposed Legal, Regulatory, and Operational Structure for an Investment-Based Social Security System. February 19, 2002

Bryson, Bill, Editor—Seeing Further—Harper Press, 2010

Buchanan, James M. and Tullock, Gordon—The Calculus of Consent: Logical Foundations of Constitutional Democracy—Liberty Fund, 1999 and University of Michigan, 1962-1990

Carlson, Robert H.—biology is technology—Harvard University Press, 2010

Christensen, Clayton M.—The Innovator's Dilemma—Harper Business, by arrangement with Harvard Business School Press, 1997

Cook, Walton—Buzzword—Public Policy Press, 2001

Cook, Walton, Wigfield, David—Birthright of Freedom—First Books, 2002

Cook, Walton—Paper on Social Security Reform—1980

de Blij, Harm—Why Geography Matters—John Wiley & Sons, 1995

de Soto, Hernando—The Mystery of Capital—Basic Books, 2000
Diamond, Jared—Guns, Germs and Steel: The Fates of Human Societies—W. W. Norton & Company, 1998

D'Souza, Dinesh—The Virtue of Prosperity: Finding Values in an Age of Techno-Affluence—Free Press, 2000

Emmott, Bill—Rivals—Harcourt, 2008

Ferguson, Niall—Colossus—The Penguin Press, 2004

Ferguson, Niall—The War of the World—The Penguin Press, 2006

Ferguson, Niall—The Ascent of Money—The Penguin Press, 2008

Friedman, Benjamin M.—The Moral Consequences of Economic Growth—Knopf, 2005

Friedman, David—Hidden Order—Harper Business, 1996

Friedman, Milton—Capitalism and Freedom—University of Chicago Press, 1962

Fukuyama, Francis—The End of History and the Last Man —Free Press, 199

Fukuyama, Francis—Trust: The Social Virtues & The Creation of Prosperity—Free Press, 1995

Gilder, George—Wealth and Poverty—Basic Books, 1981

Gladwell, Malcolm—The Tipping Point—Back Bay Books, Paperback Edition, 2002

Gleick, James—The Information—Pantheon Books, 2011

Greider, William—One World, Ready or Not—A Touchstone Book, Published by Simon and Schuster, 1997

Handy, Charles—The Hungry Spirit: Beyond Capitalism, A Quest for Purpose in the Modern World—Broadway Books, 1998

Harford, Tim—The Undercover Economist—Oxford, 2006

Harris, Judith Rich, The Nurture Assumption: Why Children Turn Out the Way They Do, Free Press, 1995

Harris, Judith Rich, No Two Alike: Human Nature and Human Individuality, Norton, 2008

Harrison, Lawrence E. and Huntington, Samuel P., Editors—Culture Matters: How Values Shape Human Progress—Basic Books.

Huntington, Samuel P.—The Clash of Civilizations and the Remaking of World Order—A Touchstone Book: Simon and Schuster, 1997

Johnson, Steven—Where Good Ideas Come From—Riverhead Books, 2010

Kelso, Louis O. and Adler, Mortimer J.—The Capitalist Manifesto—Random House, 1958

Kotlikoff, Laurence J.—Jimmy Stewart is Dead—Wiley, 2010

Landes, David S.—The Wealth and Poverty of Nations—W. W. Norton & Company, 1998, 1999

Leffler, Melvyn P. & Legro, Jeffrey W., Editors—To Lead the World—Oxford, 2008

Lindsey, Brink—Against the Dead Hand: The Uncertain Struggle for Global Capitalism—John Wiley and Sons, Inc. 2002

Lippman, Walter—A Preface to Morals—Time-Life Books, 1964

Liviris, Andrew N.—Make it in America—Wiley, 2011

Lomberg, Bjorn—Global Crises, Global Solutions, Second Edition—Cambridge University Press, 2009

Mead, Walter Russell—God and Gold—Knopf, 2007

Micklethwait, John and Wooldridge, Adrian—A Future Perfect: The Challenge and Hidden Promise of Globalization—Crown Business, 2000

Morris, Ian—Why the West Rules—For Now—Farrar, Straus & Giroux, 2010

Naim, Moises—Illicit—Doubleday, 2005

Nocera, Joseph—A Piece of the Action: How the Middle Class Joined the Money Class—Simon and Schuster, 1994

Novak, Michael—The Spirit of Democratic Capitalism—Madison Books, 1982, 1981

Novak, Michael—Freedom With Justice—Harper and Row, 1984

Novak, Michael—Edited by Brian C. Anderson. On Cultivating Liberty: Reflections on Moral Ecology—Bowman and Littlefield Publishers, Inc. 1999

Nowak, Martin A.—Super Cooperators: Altruism, Evolution, and Why We Need Each Other to Succeed, Free Press, 2011

Nye, Joseph S. Jr, Zelikow, Philip D, King, David C. Editors—Why People Don't Trust Government—Harvard, 1997

Nye, Joseph S. Jr.—The Paradox of American Power—Oxford, 2002

Nye, Joseph S. Jr.—The Powers to Lead—Oxford, 2008

Nye, Joseph S. Jr.—The Future of Power—Public Affairs, 2011

Olson, Mancur—Power and Prosperity—Basic Books, 2000

Ortega y Gasset, Jose—Revolt of the Masses—W.W. Norton & Company, 1932

Pinker, Steven—The Blank Slate—Viking, 2002

Pinker, Steven—The Stuff of Thought—Viking, 2007

Putnam, Robert D., Editor—Democracies in Flux—Oxford, 2002

Reeves, Byron and Read, J. Leighton—Total Engagement—Harvard Business Press, 2009

Reinhart, Carmen M. and Rogoff, Kenneth S.—This Time is Different—Princeton University Press, 2009

Rodrik, Dani—The Globalization Paradox—Norton, 2011

Rosecrance, Richard—The Rise of the Virtual State: Wealth and Power in the Coming Century—Basic Books, 1999

Rosenberg, Tina—Join the Club: How Peer Pressure Can Transform the World, Norton, 2011

Rossiter, Clinton & Lare, James, Editors—The Essential Lippmann—Random House, 1963

Samuelson, Robert J.—The Good Life and its Discontents—Vintage Books Edition, 1997

Schoenfeld, Gabriel—Necessary Secrets—Norton, 2010

Sen, Amaryta—Development as Freedom—Anchor Books: A Division of Random House, 1999

Simon, William E.—Correspondence to Walton Cook, 1980

Smith, Adam—A Theory of Moral Sentiments—Liberty Classics Edition, 1976. Originally published in 1759

Smith, Hedrick—Rethinking America—Avon Books, 1995

Sowell, Thomas—Knowledge and Decisions—Basic Books, 1980, 1996

Steel, Ronald—Walter Lippman and The American Century—Little Brown and Company, 1980

Wanniski, Jude—The Way the World Works—Regnery Publishing, 1982

Warsh, David—Knowledge and the Wealth of Nations—Norton, 2006

Woodward, Bob—Obama's Wars—Simon & Schuster, 2010

Wright, Robert—Moral Animal—Vintage Books, 1995

About the Author

Walton Cook is the author of the political bio-thriller, *Buzzword*, published in 2001, three months before 9/11. *Buzzword* is the world's first book on the control of narcotics producing plants and their revenues, specifically the coca shrub and the opium poppy. He also wrote *Birthright of Freedom*, with David Wigfield, CPA.

Mr. Cook is a thirty-year writer/producer of film and video. He has won both national and international awards, including the Cine Golden Eagle. These films include *"Race Against Time,"* with noted author Tom Peters; *"Amusement Park,"* a film on problems of aging, directed by the well revered George Romero; *"Challenge of Manufacturing,"* on manufacturing careers for SME; *"Come Work With Us,"* on hiring the handicapped, and major network TV sports documentaries: *"The Steel Curtain"* (Pittsburgh Steelers Front Four) *"Thank God, I'm a Country Boy"* (Terry Bradshaw) and *"I'm Back: The Rocky Bleier Story."* He is a graduate of Penn State University, majoring in political science. He writes today about social and political issues.

www.ingramcontent.com/pod-product-compliance
Lightning Source LLC
Chambersburg PA
CBHW070505200326
41519CB00013B/2717